Barbecues

BLOOMSBURY KITCHEN LIBRARY

Barbecues

Bloomsbury Books

This edition published 1995 by Bloomsbury Books,
an imprint of The Godfrey Cave Group,
42 Bloomsbury Street, London, WC1B 3QJ.

ISBN 1 85471 567 4

Printed and bound in Great Britain

Contents

Citrus-Marinated Rump Steak 7
Chicken Drumsticks in Barbecue Sauce 8
Toasted Onion Dip 9
Coriander Pork Skewers 10
Kibbeh with Yogurt-Mint Sauce 11
Sea Bass Cooked with Saffron, Thyme and Lemon 12
Shark, Onion and Pepper Brochettes 13
Two-Potato Salad 14
Green Salad with Palm Hearts and Mange-Tout 15
Barbecued Squid with Hot Paprika Sauce 16
Rum-Flavoured Soft Fruit Brochettes 17
Fruit Rings Cooked in Foil 18
Barbecued Vegetables 19
Marinated Mixed Vegetables Cooked in Foil 20
Greek Vegetable, Fruit and Cheese Kebabs 21
Skewered Cheese and Tofu Patties 22
Whole Anise-Orange Turbot 23
Barbecued Tuna Steaks 24
Tarragon-Marinated Salmon with New Potatoes 25
Sesame Seafood Kebabs 26
Barbecued Fish Steaks with Red Pepper 27
Cod Steaks Topped with Tomato and Basil 28
Chicken Sausages with Ricotta and Spinach 29
Lamb Sausages with Yogurt and Thyme 30
Pork Sausages with Orange and Sage 31
Spicy Potato Sausage with Coriander 32
Yogurt Chicken Drumsticks 33
Poussins with Rum 34
Spit-Roasted Savoury Chicken 35
Bitter-Sweet Duck Breast Salad 36
Mustard-Marinated Rabbit with Brandied Peaches 37

Pork Sheftalias with Oregano 38
Piquant Pork Chops 39
Skewers of Spiced Pork, Aubergine and Pepper 40
Pork and Apple Kebabs 41
Lamb Noisettes with Tomato and Olive Relish 42
Lamb Burgers with Basil and Parmesan Sauce 43
Lamb Skewers with Plantain 44
Spit-Roasted Moroccan Lamb 45
Barbecued Escalope of Veal 46
Mustard Steaks with Yogurt Sauce Served with Salad 47
Steakburgers with Parsnips and Brown Ale 48
Shoulder of Lamb with Anchovy Stuffing 49
Tabbouleh 50
Carrots Cooked with Honey and Spices 51
Mushroom and Parsley Pâté 52
Garlic Potato Fans and Grilled Corn-on-the-Cob 53
Fruited Cabbage Salad 54
Salad of Lettuce and Nasturtium Flowers 55
Pork Rolls with Fennel 56
Chicken, Mango and Penne Salad 57
Minted Potato and Turkey Salad 58
Artichoke and Asparagus Salad 59
Pear, Fennel and Watercress Salad 60
Salad of Red Leaves, Beans and Roots 61
Mushroom Ratatouille Salad 62
Green and White Rice Salad 63
Sweet Pepper Rice Ring 64
Charcoal-Grilled Summer Salad 65
Barbecued Bananas with Raspberry Coulis 66
Baked Apples with Ginger 67
Mixed Berry Yogurt Ice 68
Fresh Fruits in a Watermelon Bowl 69
Kebabs in Tea and Ginger Marinade 70
Porkburgers 71

Citrus-Marinated Rump Steak

Serves 12

Working time: about 25 minutes

Total time: about 5 hours and 30 minutes (includes marinating)

Calories 170
Protein 24g
Cholesterol 50mg
Total fat 8g
Saturated fat 3g
Sodium 40mg

3 tbsp	fresh orange juice	**3 tbsp**
2 tbsp	fresh lime juice	**2 tbsp**
1 tsp	fresh lemon juice	**1 tsp**
2 tbsp	virgin olive oil	**2 tbsp**
1 tbsp	dried green peppercorns, coarsely crushed	**1 tbsp**
1 or 2	garlic cloves, finely chopped	**1 or 2**
1 tbsp	fresh thyme leaves, or 1 tsp dried thyme	**1 tbsp**
1 kg	rump steak, 2.5 to 4 cm (1 to 1½ inches) thick, trimmed and cut in half	**2 lb**

In a shallow, non-reactive dish that is just large enough to hold the steaks comfortably, mix together the citrus juices, olive oil, garlic, peppercorns and thyme leaves. Put the steaks into the dish and turn them over to coat both sides with the marinade. Cover the dish closely and leave the meat to marinate in the refrigerator for at least 4 hours, or overnight.

Remove the meat from the refrigerator about 1 hour before you wish to cook it. Reserving the marinade, lay the steaks on the rack over hot coals, and cook for 4 to 5 minutes on each side for medium-rare meat; increase the cooking time to 6 to 7 minutes on each side for medium to well-done meat. Baste the steaks with the marinade when you turn them.

Transfer the cooked steaks to a carving board and allow them to rest for 5 minutes. To serve, slice each steak into six portions.

Chicken Drumsticks in Barbecue Sauce

Serves 12

Working time: about 30 minutes

Total time: about 2 hours and 30 minutes

Calories 130
Protein 16g
Cholesterol 75mg
Total fat 5g
Saturated fat 2g
Sodium 95mg

1	onion, chopped	1
1	stick celery, trimmed and diced	1
1	garlic clove, crushed	1
850 g	canned tomatoes, chopped	1¾ lb
45 g	muscovado sugar	1½ oz

1 tbsp	Worcester sauce	1 tbsp
1 tsp	hot paprika	1 tsp
	freshly ground black pepper	
12	chicken drumsticks	12
	(140 g/4½ oz each)	

To make the barbecue sauce, put all the ingredients except the drumsticks in a heavy-bottomed saucepan. Cover the pan and simmer the ingredients gently for 1 hour, or until the vegetables are very tender. Remove the pan from the heat. When the mixture has cooled, purée it in a food processor. Press the purée through a sieve into a clean pan, discarding the solids which remain in the sieve. Cook the sauce, uncovered, at a hard simmer, stirring it occasionally, until it is thick and the quantity has reduced by half—about 30 minutes.

Brush the chicken drumsticks with some of the sauce and arrange them on a lightly oiled rack over hot coals. Cook the drumsticks for 10 minutes, turning them frequently and basting them with more of the sauce each time they are turned. Move the drumsticks to the outer edges of the rack and continue to cook them for another 10 to 15 minutes, again turning them frequently and basting them with the sauce.

Insert a skewer into the thickest part of the flesh of one of the drumsticks; if the juices run clear, the drumsticks are ready. Pile the cooked drumsticks on to a serving plate. Transfer the remaining barbecue sauce to a bowl and serve it with the drumsticks.

Toasted Onion Dip

Serves 12

Working time: about 30 minutes

Total time: about 2 hours and 30 minutes (includes chilling)

Calories
45
Protein
5g
Cholesterol
trace
Total fat
2g
Saturated fat
trace
Sodium
30mg

3	large Spanish onions, two coarsely chopped	**3**
175 g	low-fat ricotta cheese	**6 oz**
175 g	low-fat soft cheese	**6 oz**
6 tbsp	finely cut chives	**6 tbsp**
	freshly ground black pepper	

Preheat the oven to 190°C (375°F or Mark 5) and line a baking sheet with foil.

Put the coarsely chopped Spanish onions in a heavy-bottomed saucepan and cover them with cold water. Bring the water to the boil, cover the pan and simmer the onions gently for 30 to 40 minutes, until they are very soft and tender.

Meanwhile, cut the remaining onion into 5 mm (¼ inch) thick slices and spread them out on the baking sheet. Toast the onion slices in the oven for about 20 minutes, turning them so that they brown evenly and removing them as they brown; do not let the onions burn. Alternatively, toast the onion slices under a preheated medium-hot grill, again watching carefully to avoid burning them. Set them aside.

When the chopped onions are cooked, drain them well and allow them to cool. Transfer them to a food processor and process them to a smooth purée. Add the low-fat cheeses and process briefly to combine the ingredients. Turn the dip into a bowl.

Crumble the toasted onion slices. Reserve 1 tablespoon for garnish, and add the remainder to the bowl, with the chives and some black pepper. Gently fold them into the dip. Cover the bowl and chill the dip for at least 1 hour. Just before serving, sprinkle the dip with the reserved toasted onion.

Coriander Pork Skewers

Serves 6

Working time: about 25 minutes

Total time: about 1 hour and 30 minutes (includes marinating)

Calories 185
Protein 19g
Cholesterol 45mg
Total fat 10g
Saturated fat 3g
Sodium 120mg

3	pieces pork fillet (350 g/12 oz), each about 15cm (6 inches) long, trimmed of fat	**3**		
1	garlic clove, crushed	**1**		
2 tsp	coriander seeds, crushed	**2 tsp**		
¼ tsp	ground allspice	**¼ tsp**		

¼ tsp	paprika	**¼ tsp**
2 tbsp	safflower oil	**2 tbsp**
8 cl	dry red wine	**3 fl oz**
¼ tsp	salt	**¼ tsp**
1 tbsp	light brown sugar	**1 tbsp**

Cut each piece of meat lengthwise into four equal strips. Place the strips of meat in a large, shallow container and add the garlic, coriander, allspice, paprika and oil. Mix the ingredients together well, then cover the container and leave the meat to marinate in a cool place for at least 1 hour, or for up to 24 hours.

Thread each strip of marinated pork on to a fine wooden skewer and lay the skewers in a large, heavy, non-stick frying pan or in a heavy-bottomed roasting pan. Using a plastic spatula, scrape up any marinade remaining in the shallow container and spread it on top of the pork skewers.

Cook the skewers over medium heat for about 5 minutes, or until they are lightly browned, turning them once. In a small bowl, whisk together the wine, salt and sugar. Add this mixture to the pan, cover it, and simmer the pork skewers in the juices for 10 minutes. Transfer the skewers to a plate and continue to cook the pan juices over high heat until they have reduced to a syrupy glaze—3 to 4 minutes. Dribble the glaze over the skewers and set them aside to cool.

To transport the skewers to the picnic site, wrap them in foil or arrange them in a rigid container. Pack the skewers inside a cool box.

Kibbeh with Yogurt-Mint Sauce

Serves 6

Working time: about 25 minutes

Total time: about 1 hour and 25 minutes (includes soaking)

Calories 155
Protein 13g
Cholesterol 30mg
Total fat 6g
Saturated fat 2g
Sodium 115mg

125g	couscous	**4 oz**
¼ tbsp	safflower oil	**¼ tbsp**
1	small onion, very finely chopped	**1**
1	garlic clove, crushed	**1**
¼ tsp	ground cinnamon	**¼ tsp**
1 tsp	ground cumin	**1 tsp**
200 g	lean lamb, finely minced	**7 oz**
¼ tsp	salt	**¼ tsp**
	freshly ground black pepper	

	lemon slices, halved, for garnish	
	flat-leaf parsley sprig, for garnish	
	Yogurt-mint sauce	
15 cl	plain low-fat yogurt	**¼ pint**
1½ tbsp	chopped mint leaves, plus two mint leaves, cut into strips, for garnish	**1½ tbsp**
¼ tsp	caraway seeds	**¼ tsp**
¼	cucumber, peeled and grated	**¼**
	freshly ground black pepper	

Put the couscous in a bowl with 15 cl (¼ pint) of boiling water. Soak for 15 minutes, until the liquid has been absorbed; stir occasionally, to prevent lumps.

Heat the oil in a small frying pan. Add the onion, garlic, cinnamon and cumin, and fry gently for 2 minutes, stirring. Stir into the couscous, then stir in the lamb, the salt and some pepper. Mix together thoroughly.

Preheat the oven to 190°C (375°F or Mark 5) and lightly grease a baking sheet. Divide the meat mixture into 12. Squeeze and roll each portion into a firm ball, then place all 12 on the prepared baking sheet.

Bake for 45 minutes, until golden. Transfer to a plate to cool, then chill until required.

Combine the yogurt, chopped mint, caraway seeds and cucumber in a bowl and add a little black pepper. Chill.

To serve, arrange the kibbeh in a serving dish and garnish them with the lemon slices and parsley sprig. Serve the yogurt sauce separately in a small bowl and scatter the mint strips over the surface.

Sea Bass Cooked with Saffron, Thyme and Lemon

Serves 12

Working time: about 30 minutes

Total time: about 1 hour and 10 minutes

Calories 150

Protein 27g

Cholesterol 115mg

Total fat 3g

Saturated fat trace

Sodium 155mg

2.5 kg	sea bass, gutted and scaled	**5 lb**
1 tsp	virgin olive oil	**1 tsp**
½ tsp	powdered saffron	**½ tsp**
½ tsp	salt	**½ tsp**
	freshly ground black pepper	

1	lemon, sliced	**1**
1	large bunch thyme, stalks trimmed	**1**
	tied bundles of chives, for garnish	
	lemon slices and lime wedges, for garnish	

Rinse the fish under cold running water and pat it dry with paper towels. Make four 5 mm (¼ inch) deep slashes in the flesh on each side of the fish. Using a small pastry brush, oil each slash with a little of the olive oil and paint in some saffron powder.

Place the fish on an oiled fish basket and season the stomach cavity with the salt and some freshly ground black pepper. Place the lemon slices and the bunch of thyme in the stomach cavity, arranging them so that the natural stomach shape is retained.

Close the fish basket and place it on the barbecue rack. Cook the sea bass over medium hot coals for 20 minutes on each side, or until it is firm to the touch. Transfer the cooked fish to a large platter, and serve it garnished with the bundles of chives, the lemon slices and the lime wedges.

Shark, Onion and Pepper Brochettes

Serves 12

Working time:
about 45
minutes

Total time:
about 25 hours
(includes
marinating)

Calories
120
Protein
8g
Cholesterol
25mg
Total fat
8g
Saturated fat
2g
Sodium
85mg

2 tbsp	virgin olive oil	**2 tbsp**
8 cl	fresh lime juice	**3 fl oz**
1 tbsp	gin	**1 tbsp**
¼ tsp	salt	**¼ tsp**
200 g	baby onions, simmered in boiling water for 8 to 10 minutes, until tender	**7 oz**
750 g	shark fillet, skinned and cut into 3 cm (1¼ inch) cubes	**1½ lb**

	freshly ground black pepper	
2	sweet orange peppers, seeded, deribbed and cut into 3 cm (1¼ inch) pieces	2
2	sweet yellow peppers, seeded, deribbed and cut into 3 cm (1¼ inch) pieces	2
	bamboo leaves, for garnish (optional)	

First prepare a marinade for the cubed shark fillet. In a large, shallow, non-reactive dish, combine 1 tablespoon of the olive oil with the lime juice, gin, salt and some black pepper. Add the shark cubes to the dish and turn them over thoroughly in the marinade, to all the surfaces. Arrange the cubes in a single layer, cover the dish and place it in the refrigerator for at least 24 hours. Turn the cubes over from time to time while they are marinating.

Divide the shark cubes, baby onions and pieces of orange and yellow pepper into 12 equal portions. Thread each portion on to a long metal skewer, then brush the filled skewers with the remaining olive oil.

Place the skewers on the barbecue rack over medium-hot coals and cook them for about 10 minutes, turning them over half way through cooking. Pile the skewers on to a serving platter, lined with a few bamboo leaves, if you are using them.

Two-Potato Salad

Serves 12

Working time: about 30 minutes

Total time: about 1 hour and 15 minutes

Calories
80
Protein
2g
Cholesterol
0mg
Total fat
trace
Saturated fat
trace
Sodium
35mg

500 g	sweet potatoes, scrubbed	**1 lb**	
500 g	new potatoes, scrubbed, halved if large	**1 lb**	
250 g	spring onions, trimmed and cut diagonally into thirds	**8 oz**	
2 tsp	Dijon mustard	**2 tsp**	
15 cl	plain low-fat yogurt	**¼ pint**	
	white pepper		
2 tbsp	capers, rinsed well, dried and roughly chopped	**2 tbsp**	

Place the sweet potatoes and new potatoes into separate heavy-bottomed saucepans and pour in sufficient cold water to cover the potatoes in each pan by 2.5 cm (1 inch). Bring both pans to the boil, then reduce the heat and simmer the vegetables until they are tender—15 to 20 minutes for the new potatoes, and 25 to 30 minutes for the sweet potatoes.

Drain the potatoes and set them aside, on separate plates, until they are cool enough to handle. Peel the sweet potatoes and cut them into slices. Arrange the slices in a serving dish with the new potatoes and the spring onion pieces.

In a small bowl, stir the Dijon mustard into the yogurt and season with some white pepper. Pour this dressing over the potatoes and onions, and sprinkle the capers over the top of the salad.

Green Salad with Palm Hearts and Mange-Tout

4	little gem or other small round lettuces, cut in half, leaves washed and dried	4
650 g	canned palm hearts, rinsed well, each cut crosswise into four equal pieces	22 oz
2	cucumbers, halved lengthwise, seeded and cut into 5 cm (2 inch) long sticks	2
175 g	watercress sprigs, trimmed, washed and dried	6 oz
600 g	mange-tout, strings removed, blanched, refreshed under cold running water	1 ¼ lb
	Lemon vinaigrette	
2 tbsp	safflower oil	2 tbsp
2 tbsp	fresh lemon juice	2 tbsp
	freshly ground black pepper	

First prepare the lemon vinaigrette. In a small bowl, mix the oil and lemon juice using a fork, and season the dressing with plenty of black pepper.

Pile all the ingredients for the salad into a large bowl. Just before serving, pour on the lemon dressing and toss the salad thoroughly.

Barbecued Squid with Hot Paprika Sauce

Serves 12

Working (and
total) time:
about 1 hour

Calories
75

Protein
9g

Cholesterol
130mg

Total fat
3g

Saturated fat
1g

Sodium
95mg

750g	squid, cleaned and skinned, tentacles reserved	**1 ½ lb**	
48	small button mushrooms, wiped	**48**	
	Hot paprika sauce		
2 tbsp	virgin olive oil	**2 tbsp**	
500g	ripe tomatoes, skinned, seeded and chopped	**1 lb**	

1	garlic clove, crushed	**1**
2 tsp	red wine vinegar	**2 tsp**
2 tsp	paprika	**2 tsp**
1 tsp	Tabasco sauce	**1 tsp**
175g	canned red pimentos, roughly chopped	**6oz**

First make the sauce. In a heavy frying pan, heat the oil over medium heat. Add the garlic and tomatoes and cook them, stirring constantly, for 10 minutes. Strain off and discard 30 cl (½ pint) of the juice. Add the vinegar to the pan and simmer the mixture over low heat for a further 3 minutes. Pour the mixture into a food processor or blender, add the remaining ingredients, and process until smooth. Transfer to a bowl and set aside.

Cut each squid pouch into three or four pieces and the tentacles into groups of four. Thread the squid and mushrooms on to skewers. Place the skewers flat on the rack of the barbecue, spreading out the squid tentacles. Cook the skewers for 5 minutes on each side, until golden-brown. Remove the squid and mushrooms from their skewers and mix them on a platter. Serve the bowl of sauce separately.

Rum-Flavoured Soft Fruit Brochettes

Serves 6

Working time: about 20 minutes

Total time: about 30 minutes

Calories 125
Protein 1g
Cholesterol 0mg
Total fat trace
Saturated fat trace
Sodium 5mg

3 tbsp	dark rum	**3 tbsp**
3 tbsp	light brown sugar	**3 tbsp**
2 tbsp	fresh lemon juice	**2 tbsp**
3	kiwi fruit, peeled and quartered	**3**
6	dark-skinned plums, halved and stoned	**6**
3	small nectarines, quartered	**3**
2	bananas, peeled, each cut into six chunks	**2**
12	strawberries, hulled	**12**
1	orange, juice only	**1**
1 tbsp	clear honey	**1 tbsp**

Put the rum, sugar and lemon juice in a large, shallow dish. Add the kiwi fruit, plums, nectarines and bananas to the liquid, and turn them to coat them evenly. Leave the fruits to marinate for about 10 minutes. Meanwhile, soak six bamboo skewers in water for 10 minutes. Juxtaposing different fruits, thread two strawberries and two pieces of each of the other fruits on to each of the skewers; reserve the marinade. Set the skewers aside while you prepare a rum sauce.

Pour the marinade into a small pan and stir in the orange juice and honey. Bring the sauce slowly to the boil, and boil it until it is reduced by half—about 5 minutes. Set the sauce aside to cool.

Lightly oil the barbecue rack. Brush the kebabs with a little of the rum sauce and cook them over medium-hot coals for 4 minutes, turning them once. Serve the fruit kebabs immediately with any remaining rum sauce poured over them.

Editor's Note: Any soft fruit, such as orange, grapefruit, peach or mango, may be substituted for those listed above.

Fruit Rings Cooked in Foil

Serves 6

Working (and total) time: about 30 minutes

Calories
85
Protein
1g
Cholesterol
0mg
Total fat
0g
Saturated fat
0g
Sodium
5mg

2	red-skinned apples, cored, each cut into six rings and dropped into acidulated water	**2**		
2	ripe pears, peeled, cored, each cut into six rings and dropped into acidulated water	**2**		
2	oranges, peeled, each cut crosswise into six slices	**2**		
1	grapefruit, peeled and cut crosswise into six slices	**1**		
2 tbsp	light brown sugar	**2 tbsp**		

Cut six rectangles of foil measuring about 45 by 30 cm (18 by 12 inches), and fold them in half crosswise.

Drain the apple and pear rings. In the centre of each rectangle of foil, pile two rings each of apple, pear and orange, and one slice of grapefruit. Sprinkle 1 teaspoon of sugar over each pile of fruit, then fold the sides of the foil up and pinch the edges to enclose the fruit in six neat parcels.

Put the parcels on the grid over medium-hot coals and cook for 4 minutes. Serve hot, in the parcels, or on individual plates with the juices poured over.

Barbecued Vegetables

Serves 24

Working time:
about 40
minutes

Total time:
about 1 hour
and 40
minutes
(includes
marinating)

Calories
50
Protein
1g
Cholesterol
0mg
Total fat
4g
Saturated fat
1g
Sodium
50mg

48	shallots, blanched	**48**
3	fennel bulbs, halved, blanched	**3**
10	baby sweetcorn, trimmed, blanched	**10**
24	cherry tomatoes, stalks removed	**24**
4	sweet green peppers	**4**
4	sweet yellow peppers	**4**
2 tbsp	safflower oil	**2 tbsp**
3	red onions. halved	**3**
3	white onions halved	**3**
	Marinade for shallots	
1 tbsp	virgin olive oil	**1 tbsp**

1 tbsp	fresh lemon juice	**1 tbsp**
1 tbsp	very finely chopped parsley	**1 tbsp**
⅛ tsp	salt	**⅛ tsp**
	white pepper	
	Marinade for fennel	
1 tbsp	virgin olive oil	**1 tbsp**
1	garlic clove, crushed	**1**
1 tbsp	chopped fresh marjoram	**1 tbsp**
⅛ tsp	salt	**⅛ tsp**
	white pepper	

Mix together the ingredients for the shallot marinade. Add the shallots, and stir them to coat them thoroughly. Cover and marinate for 1 hour.

Mix together the ingredients for the fennel marinade. Lay the fennel in a shallow dish and brush on the marinade. Cover for 1 hour.

Thread the sweetcorn and cherry tomatoes alternately on to skewers. Thread the shallots on to separate skewers.

Brush the peppers with safflower oil and place on the barbecue rack. Cook for 20 to 25 minutes over medium-hot coals, turning until blistered and tender. After 10 minutes, place the onions and the fennel on the grid. Brush the onions with oil, and the fennel with any remaining marinade. Cook for 10 to 15 minutes, turning once, until lightly browned and tender.

Five to 10 minutes before these vegetables are ready, place the shallots, tomatoes and sweetcorn on the barbecue; turn twice during cooking. Move the vegetables to the edges of the barbecue as they finish cooking.

Marinated Mixed Vegetables Cooked in Foil

Serves 6

Working time:
about 35
minutes

Total time:
about 2 hours
and 15
minutes

Calories
75

Protein
2g

Cholesterol
0mg

Total fat
5g

Saturated fat
1g

Sodium
45mg

1	small aubergine, sliced thickly	1
1 tbsp	salt	1 tbsp
1 tbsp	fresh lemon juice	1 tbsp
175 g	small young okra	6 oz
1	small fennel bulb, cut into six wedges, feathery top chopped	1
175 g	courgettes, sliced thinly	6 oz
1	sweet red pepper, seeded, cut into 12 strips	1
1	sweet orange pepper, seeded, cut into 12 strips	1

Herb and lemon marinade

2 tbsp	virgin olive oil	2 tbsp
12	small shallots	12
1	garlic clove	1
6	sun-dried tomatoes, quartered	6
1	lemon, juice only	1
1½ tsp	chopped parsley	1½ tsp
1½ tsp	fresh thyme leaves	1½ tsp
1½ tsp	chopped fresh oregano	1½ tsp
2	stoned black olives, cut into rings	2
¼ tsp	salt	¼ tsp
	freshly ground black pepper	

Place the aubergine in a colander, sprinkle on the salt, and drain for 30 minutes. Rinse thoroughly and pat them dry.

Add the okra and lemon juice to a pan of boiling water. Cook for 5 seconds, add the fennel and cook for 10 secs. Drain and refresh the vegetables. Halve the okra lengthwise. Put all the vegetables in a large bowl.

Heat the oil gently in a pan and fry the shallots until golden-brown. Add the garlic and fry for 20 secs, then remove from the heat. Stir in the tomatoes and leave for 15 minutes. Add the remaining marinade ingredients and fennel top. Pour over the vegetables, toss gently and cover. Marinate for at least 1 hour, or overnight in the refrigerator, turning several times.

Divide the vegetables into six portions and wrap each in a double-thickness foil parcel. Cook over medium-hot coals for 20 to 30 minutes. Unwrap and serve.

Greek Vegetable, Fruit and Cheese Kebabs

Serves 8

Working time:
about 1 hour

Total time:
about 2 hours

Calories
170

Protein
7g

Cholesterol
25mg

Total fat
10g

Saturated fat
5g

Sodium
335mg

125 g	aubergine, cut into eight 2.5 cm (1 inch) cubes	**4 oz**
¼ tsp	salt	**¼ tsp**
8	new potatoes (350 g/12 oz), scrubbed	**8**
2	onions, quartered	**2**
2	sweet red or orange peppers, seeded, each cut into eight squares	**2**
1	small cucumber, cut into eight thick slices	**1**
8	large button mushrooms, wiped clean	**8**

200 g	halloumi or feta cheese, cut into eight cubes	**7 oz**
2	nectarines, quartered and stoned	**2**
2 tbsp	virgin olive oil	**2 tbsp**
	fresh vine leaves, for garnish (optional)	
	Minted sauce	
30 cl	plain low-fat yogurt	**½ pint**
3 tbsp	chopped mint	**3 tbsp**
1	garlic clove, crushed	**1**

Sprinkle the aubergine with the salt and set aside for 30 minutes. Cook the potatoes and onions in simmering water for 15 to 20 minutes. Drain and leave to cool.

Rinse the aubergine and put it in a pan of boiling water. Boil, then reduce the heat and simmer for 2 minutes. Add the cucumber, cook for 1 min, then add the peppers and cook for 2 minutes. Drain and cool.

Combine the yogurt, mint, and garlic in a serving bowl. Put the vegetables, mushrooms, nectarines and cheese on a tray and sprinkle with oil. Lightly oil eight metal skewers; thread with one of each item. Oil the rack and cook over hot coals for about 15 minutes, turning frequently, until tender and lightly charred.

Serve the kebabs at once, on platters lined with vine leaves, accompanied by the sauce.

Skewered Cheese and Tofu Patties

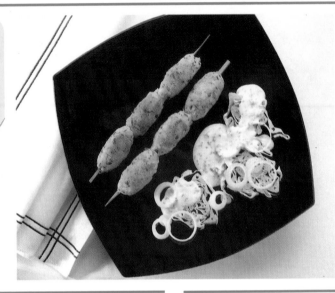

Serves 4

Working time: about 45 minutes

Total time: about 55 minutes

Calories 240
Protein 15g
Cholesterol 30mg
Total fat 12g
Saturated fat 5g
Sodium 435mg

1 tsp	safflower oil	1 tsp
125 g	onion, finely chopped	4 oz
90 g	fresh white breadcrumbs	3 oz
250 g	smoked tofu	8 oz
125 g	Edam cheese, coarsely grated	4 oz

$\frac{1}{4}$ tsp	freshly ground black pepper	$\frac{1}{4}$ tsp
$\frac{1}{2}$ tsp	dry mustard	$\frac{1}{2}$ tsp
2 tbsp	chopped parsley	2 tbsp
12	sage leaves, roughly chopped	12
2 tbsp	plain flour	2 tbsp

Soak eight bamboo skewers in water for 10 minutes.

Meanwhile, heat the oil in a small, non-stick frying pan. Add the onion and cook it over medium heat until it is transparent—about 8 minutes. Stir in the breadcrumbs. Remove the pan from the heat and let the mixture cool. Chop the tofu finely in a food processor, then add the cheese, pepper, mustard, parsley and sage. Add the breadcrumb mixture and process briefly, until all the ingredients are evenly combined.

Divide the mixture into 24 equal portions. Mould each portion into a small barrel-shaped patty. Thread these patties on to the bamboo

skewers: take a patty in one hand and thread a skewer gently through it lengthwise, holding it firmly in shape as you do so. Keep the remaining patties covered with a damp cloth while you are working, to prevent them from drying out. Sprinkle the flour on the work surface and carefully roll the skewers in it, so that all the patties are coated evenly in flour; brush off any excess flour.

Place a griddle or baking sheet on the barbecue and brush it lightly with oil. Arrange the skewers on the griddle and cook the patties for 6 to 8 minutes, turning them frequently, until they are golden-brown all over. Serve the cheese and tofu patties immediately.

Whole Anise-Orange Turbot

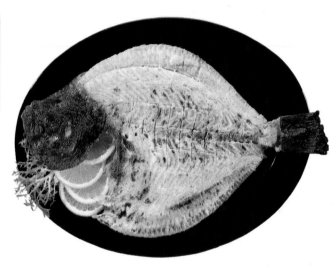

Serves 4

Working (and total) time: about 25 minutes

Calories 250
Protein 20g
Cholesterol 80mg
Total fat 15g
Saturated fat 4g
Sodium 125mg

1½ tsp	ground fennel seeds	**1½ tsp**
1	whole turbot (1.5 kg/3 ¼ lb), gilled and bled	**1**
100 g	thick Greek yogurt	**3½ oz**
⅛ tsp	salt	**⅛ tsp**
⅛ tsp	white pepper	**⅛ tsp**

1	orange, four slices reserved for garnish, ½ tsp finely grated rind and peel of remainder	**1**
6	dried fennel stalks	**6**
2 tsp	Pernod	**2 tsp**
	curly endive leaves, for garnish	

Sprinkle a little of the ground fennel in the gill cavity of the turbot. Mix the yogurt, orange rind, salt and pepper with remaining ground fennel, and set aside.

Grill the fish, dark skin side down, on an oiled barbecue rack over hot coals for 2½ minutes. Remove and place on a work surface. Cut the skin free at the tail and head ends. Strip off all the dark skin. Return the fish to the barbecue, white skin side down, and grill for about 1½ minutes. Remove from the barbecue and strip off the white skin.

Lightly oil a grilling basket. Coat one side of the fish with half of the yogurt mixture, and place it, coated side down, on the grilling basket. Spread the remaining yogurt mixture over the second side of the turbot. Close the basket and place the fish on the barbecue with the thick side down. Grill for 2 minutes, then turn and grill for 1 minute. Repeat this process twice more. Throw the orange peel and fennel stalks on to the coals. Pour 1 teaspoon of pernod over the thick side of the fish and grill it for 2 minutes. Turn and pour the remaining teaspoon of spirit over the thin side. Grill for 1 minute. The flesh should be opaque all over and flake easily from the bone. test the fish at its thickest part with a small knife. Grill it for a little longer if necessary, but do not overcook it. Serve at once, garnished with the orange slices and curly endive leaves.

Barbecued Tuna Steaks

Serves 6

Working time: about 30 minutes

Total time: about 5 hours (includes marinating)

Calories 275

Protein 35g

Cholesterol 80mg

Total fat 16g

Saturated fat 5g

Sodium 105mg

3	tuna steaks (about 250 g/8 oz)	**3**
8	spring onions, chopped	**8**
5 cm	piece fresh ginger root, grated	**2 inch**
4	garlic cloves	**4**
1	large onion, chopped	**1**
1	lime, juice only	**1**

4 tbsp	white wine vinegar	**4 tbsp**
2 tbsp	virgin olive oil	**2 tbsp**
1 tsp	finely crushed black peppercorns	**1 tsp**
$\frac{1}{8}$ tsp	salt	**$\frac{1}{8}$ tsp**
200 g	fromage frais	**7 oz**
	lime slices, for garnish	

Cut the tuna steaks in half and remove the bone from the middle of each steak. Place the fish in a shallow dish and set it aside while you make the marinade.

Put the spring onions, grated ginger root, garlic cloves and chopped onion in a food processor or blender. Add the lime juice, wine vinegar and olive oil, and process the ingredients to a smooth purée. Stir the crushed peppercorns and the salt into the purée, then pour two thirds of it over the tuna pieces, coating them evenly; reserve the remaining marinade for use in the sauce. Cover the tuna pieces and leave them to marinate in the refrigerator for at least 3 hours, or up to 12

hours. Remove them from the refrigerator at least 1 hour before they are to be cooked, to allow them to reach room temperature.

Soak six bamboo skewers in water for 10 minutes. Thread one skewer through each piece of tuna about 2.5 cm (1 inch) from the straight, cut, edge, to keep it flat as it cooks. Cook the tuna over hot coals for 5 to 6 minutes on each side, until it is lightly browned and cooked through.

While the tuna is cooking, stir the remaining marinade into the *fromage frais*. Remove the skewers from the tuna pieces. Serve the tuna with the *fromage frais* sauce, garnished with lime slices.

Tarragon-Marinated Salmon with New Potatoes

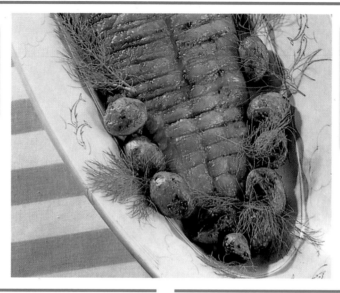

Serves 8

Working time:
about 1 hour

Total time:
about 14 hours
(includes
marinating)

Calories
305

Protein
26g

Cholesterol
85mg

Total fat
17g

Saturated fat
4g

Sodium
395mg

1 kg	salmon fillet	**2¼ lb**
15 g	fresh tarragon, chopped	**½ oz**
15 g	salt	**½ oz**
30 g	light brown sugar	**1 oz**
1 tbsp	vodka	**1 tbsp**
1½ tsp	crushed black peppercorns	**1½ tsp**

350 g	small new potatoes	**12 oz**
1 tsp	grapeseed or safflower oil	**1 tsp**
	dried fennel twigs or seeds,	
	to burn on the barbecue	
	fennel leaves, for garnish	

Wipe the salmon, remove remaining small bones with tweezers. Lay the salmon in a large, shallow dish. Mix the tarragon, salt, sugar, vodka and 1 teaspoon peppercorns. Using the back of a metal spoon, spread this tarragon marinade over the flesh side of the salmon. Cover loosely with a damp cloth, and marinate in the refrigerator for at least 12 hours.

Soak several bamboo skewers in cold water for 10 minutes. Cook the new potatoes in boiling water until they are just tender—10 to 15 minutes. Drain the potatoes and return them to the saucepan. Add the grapeseed oil and the remaining peppercorns, and toss the potatoes to coat them evenly. Thread the potatoes on to the skewers, and set aside.

Lightly oil the barbecue rack. Wipe the salmon and cook it, flesh side down, over hot coals for 1 min. Turn over and grill for a further 6 to 9 minutes, until almost cooked through but not quite opaque near the bone. After about 3 minutes, place the potatoes on the grid and heat them until browned. Throw the dried fennel on to the coals.

Transfer the salmon to a serving platter. Arrange the new potatoes round and garnish with fennel leaves.

Sesame Seafood Kebabs

Serves 4

Working time:
about 30
minutes

Total time:
about 1 hour
and 30
minutes

Calories
195
Protein
21g
Cholesterol
85mg
Total fat
7g
Saturated fat
3g
Sodium
130mg

¼ litre	dry white wine	8 fl oz	1 tsp	cornflour	1 tsp
1 tbsp	safflower oil	1 tbsp	1 tbsp	chopped mixed fresh herbs, such as basil, parsley and chives	1 tbsp
1	garlic clove, crushed	1	1 tbsp	toasted sesame seeds	1 tbsp
½	lemon grated rind and 1 tbsp juice	½	4	large raw prawns	4
⅛ tsp	salt	⅛ tsp	8	scallops, bright white connective tissue removed	8
	freshly ground black pepper			shredded lettuce for garnish	
350 g	monkfish fillets	12 oz			

Mix 15 cl (¼ pint) of the wine with the oil, garlic, lemon rind and juice, salt and some pepper. Pour half into a small pan. Cut the fish into 12 and add to the wine mixture remaining in the bowl. Turn the pieces over to coat thoroughly. Cover and refrigerate for 1 to 2 hours.

Add the remaining wine to the saucepan. Blend the cornflour with a little cold water. Stir into the pan and heat it slowly, stirring continuously, until it boils and thickens. Remove from the heat, then stir in the mixed herbs and sesame seeds. Cover the pan and keep it warm on a low heat.

Lightly oil four skewers. Drain the fish and thread on to the skewers, alternating with prawns and scallops. Cook over medium-hot coals for 3 to 5 minutes on each side; turn them gently.

Spread the shredded lettuce on a large platter and pour the sauce into a warmed jug. Arrange the kebabs on the shredded lettuce and serve immediately, accompanied by the sauce.

Editor's Note: To toast sesame seeds, sprinkle a layer of seeds in a heavy-bottomed pan, cover, and cook over high heat. When they begin to pop, keep the pan on the heat for 1 minute more but shake it constantly.

Barbecued Fish Steaks with Red Pepper

Serves 4

Working time: about 45 minutes

Total time: about 1 hour

Calories 215

Protein 27g

Cholesterol 75mg

Total fat 12g

Saturated fat 2g

Sodium 215mg

600 g	grouper or cod fillets, skin left on, cut into four pieces	**1¼ lb**
2	limes, juice of one, the other cut into wedges, for garnish	**2**
1¼ tbsp	virgin olive oil	**1¼ tbsp**
½ tsp	salt	**½ tsp**
	freshly ground black pepper	
2	large sweet red peppers	**2**

Put the fish pieces, skin side down, in a shallow dish. In a small bowl, combine the olive oil, lime juice, salt and some freshly ground black pepper. Reserve 1 tablespoon of this marinade and brush the remainder on the upper side of the steaks. Set the fish aside, covered, to marinate for 30 minutes.

Meanwhile, place the red peppers on the barbecue rack over hot coals. Cook them for 10 to 15 minutes, turning them frequently, until their skins blacken. Remove the cooked peppers from the barbecue and allow them to cool. When they are cool enough to handle, peel off their skins. Slice the skinned peppers thinly and evenly. Toss the slices in the reserved marinade, and set them aside.

Place the fish in an oiled grilling basket and grill it, skin side down, over low coals, for 10 to 15 minutes. Turn the fish over and cook it for a further 5 minutes. Serve the fish immediately, accompanied by the red pepper strips and garnished with the lime wedges.

Cod Steaks Topped with Tomato and Basil

Serves 4

Working time:
about 20
minutes

Total time:
about 30
minutes

Calories
170
Protein
27g
Cholesterol
75mg
Total fat
4g
Saturated fat
1g
Sodium
120mg

500 g	tomatoes, skinned, seeded and chopped	**1 lb**
20 g	basil leaves, chopped	**¾ oz**
3 tbsp	medium-dry sherry	**3 tbsp**
½ tsp	salt	**½ tsp**

	freshly ground black pepper	
2 tsp	virgin olive oil	**2 tsp**
4	cod steaks (about 150 g/5 oz each), central bones removed	**4**

In a bowl, mix the chopped tomatoes with the basil and sherry, and season the mixture with the salt and some freshly ground black pepper. Brush the olive oil over four double-thickness rectangles of foil, each one measuring about 32 by 20 cm (13 by 8 inches). Lay a cod steak on each piece of foil and top it with a quarter of the tomato mixture. Wrap the foil round the fish steaks, sealing the edges securely to keep all the cooking juices in the packets.

Cook the cod steaks over hot coals for 3 to 5 minutes on each side, taking care not to split the foil when turning the packets over. Unwrap the packets with the tomato side up and slide the contents of each one on to an individual plate. Remove and discard the thin strips of cod skin and serve the steaks at once.

Chicken Sausages with Ricotta and Spinach

Makes 12
sausages

Working time:
about 1 hour

Total time:
about 1 hour
and 15
minutes

Per sausage:
Calories
105
Protein
16g
Cholesterol
45mg
Total fat
3g
Saturated fat
1g
Sodium
160mg

125 g	spinach, washed, centre stems removed	**4 oz**
45 g	sorrel, washed, centre stems removed	**1¼ oz**
675 g	chicken (leg or thigh), minced	**1 lb 6 oz**
175 g	low-fat ricotta cheese	**6 oz**
4	shallots, finely chopped	**4**

1 tbsp	chopped parsley	**1 tbsp**
1 tbsp	chopped fresh tarragon	**1 tbsp**
¾ tsp	salt	**¾ tsp**
	freshly ground black pepper	
125 g	low-fat fromage frais	**4 oz**
2 metres	lamb sausage casings, soaked	**7 feet**

Blanch the spinach and sorrel, and refresh them under cold water; drain and chop them. Wrap them in a piece of muslin or paper towel, squeeze them dry and place them in a bowl. Mix in the chicken, ricotta, shallots, herbs, salt, some pepper and half of the *fromage frais*. Add more *fromage frais* until the mixture is loose enough to be squeezed

through a piping bag but stiff enough to be moulded into a walnut-sized ball.

Fill the casings with the mixture and form links. Cut between the links to separate the sausages. Prick each sausage several times. Oil the barbecue rack lightly and cook the sausages over medium-hot coals for 10 to 15 minutes, until golden-brown, turning frequently.

Lamb Sausages with Yogurt and Thyme

Makes 12
sausages

Working time:
about 1 hour

Total time:
about 1 hour
and 15
minutes

Per sausage:
Calories
135
Protein
16g
Cholesterol
40mg
Total fat
6g
Saturated fat
5g
Sodium
175mg

60 g	couscous	**2 oz**	**1**	onion, finely chopped		**1**
675 g	lean leg of lamb, trimmed of fat and minced	**1 lb 6 oz**	**2**	garlic cloves, finely chopped		**2**
150 g	thick Greek ewe's milk yogurt	**5 oz**	**4**	black olives, stoned, finely diced		**4**
1 tbsp	virgin olive oil	**1 tbsp**	**$\frac{3}{4}$ tsp**	salt		**$\frac{3}{4}$ tsp**
175 g	sweet red or orange pepper, peeled and finely diced	**6 oz**		freshly ground black pepper		
1$\frac{1}{2}$ tbsp	fresh thyme leaves	**1$\frac{1}{2}$ tbsp**	**2 metres**	lamb sausage casings, soaked		**7 feet**

First soak the couscous in 10 cl (3$\frac{1}{2}$ fl oz) of water for 10 to 15 minutes, until it has absorbed all the water. Place the soaked conscious in a piece of muslin or paper towel and squeeze out as much water as possible. Place the couscous in a large bowl. Add the lamb, yogurt, olive oil, sweet pepper, thyme, onion, garlic, olives, salt and some black pepper, and mix them well.

Fill the lamb sausage casings with the mixture and form links. Cut between the links to separate the sausages. Prick each sausage several times. Oil the barbecue rack lightly and cook the sausages over medium-hot coals for 10 to 15 minutes, until golden-brown, turning them frequently.

Pork Sausages with Orange and Sage

Makes 12
sausages

Working time:
about 1 hour

Total time:
about 1 hour
and 15
minutes

Per sausage:
Calories
170
Protein
20g
Cholesterol
45mg,
Total fat
8g
Saturated fat
4g
Sodium
325 mg

750 g	neck end of pork, trimmed of excess fat, coarsely chopped	**1½ lb**
125 g	lean bacon, trimmed of fat and finely diced	**4 oz**
4 tsp	grated orange rind	**4 tsp**
2 tbsp	shredded fresh sage leaves	**2 tbsp**
1	onion, finely chopped	**1**
1	garlic clove, finely chopped	**1**
1 tsp	ground ginger	**1 tsp**
¾ tsp	salt	**¾ tsp**

	white pepper	
2 tbsp	red vermouth or sherry	**2 tbsp**
1½ tsp	orange-flavoured liqueur or brandy	**1½ tsp**
2 tbsp	fresh orange juice	**2 tbsp**
100 g	fresh breadcrumbs	**3½ oz**
2 metres	lamb sausage casings, soaked	**7 feet**
4 tbsp	unsalted chicken stock, reduced by boiling to 2 tbsp	**4 tbsp**

In a bowl, blend together all of the ingredients except for the casings and 1 tablespoon of the reduced stock. Gradually blend in some or all of the remaining stock until the mixture is loose enough to be squeezed through a piping bag but stiff enough to be moulded into a walnut-sized ball.

Fill the casings with the stuffing and form links. Cut between the links to separate the sausages. Prick each sausage several times. Oil the barbecue rack lightly and cook the sausages over medium-hot coals for 10 to 15 minutes, turning them frequently, until they are golden-brown.

Spicy Potato Sausage with Coriander

Makes 12
sausages

Working time:
about 1 hour

Total time:
about 2 hours

Per sausage:
Calories
75
Protein
3g
Cholesterol
20mg
Total fat
2g
Saturated fat
1g
Sodium
140mg

15 g	unsalted butter	**½ oz**	**1 tsp**	mustard seeds. toasted	**1 tsp**
1	large onion, finely chopped	**1**	**1½ tbsp**	cut chives	**1½ tbsp**
300 g	mushrooms, finely chopped	**10 oz**	**1½ tbsp**	chopped fresh coriander	**1½ tbsp**
1 or 2	garlic cloves, finely chopped	**1 or 2**	**¾ tsp**	salt	**¾ tsp**
3 cm	piece fresh ginger root, finely chopped	**1½ inch**	**¼ tsp**	cayenne pepper	**¼ tsp**
				freshly ground black pepper	
750 g	potatoes, boiled and mashed	**1½ lb**	**100 g**	fromage frais	**3 oz**
1	egg, plus one egg white	**1**	**2 metres**	lamb sausage casings, soaked	**7 feet**
1 tsp	poppy seeds	**1 tsp**			

Melt the butter in a pan and fry the onion over medium heat until it is soft—about 5 minutes. Increase the heat, add the mushrooms, garlic and ginger, and fry until the mixture is quite dry—about 3 minutes.

Place the potatoes in a bowl over a pan of simmering water. Add the egg and egg white and stir until the egg thickens. Remove the bowl from the heat and stir in the onion mixture, and all the remaining ingredients except for the casings. Cool, then chill the filling.

Fill the casings with the mixture and form links. Cut between the links to separate the sausages. Prick each of the sausages several times. Oil the barbecue rack lightly and cook the sausages gently for 15 to 20 minutes, turning several times, until golden-brown.

Yogurt Chicken Drumsticks

Serves 8

Working time:
about 30 minutes

Total time:
about 3 hours and 30 minutes (includes marinating)

Calories
160
Protein
26g
Cholesterol
90mg
Total fat
6g
Saturated fat
2g
Sodium
190mg

16	chicken drumsticks (about 1.5 kg/3 lb), skinned	**16**
½ tsp	salt	**½ tsp**
1	lemon, grated rind and juice	**1**
3 tbsp	paprika	**3 tbsp**
½ tsp	Tabasco sauce	**½ tsp**
15 cl	plain low-fat yogurt	**¼ pint**
	freshly ground black pepper	
	crisp salad leaves, for garnish	

Cut two deep, diagonal slits in opposite sides of each drumstick. In a small bowl, stir the salt and the grated lemon rind into the lemon juice, then rub the mixture over each drumstick and into the slits. Place the drumsticks on a wire rack set over a baking tray, and sieve 1 tablespoon of the paprika evenly over the upper side of the drumsticks.

In another bowl, mix together the Tabasco sauce, yogurt and some black pepper. Using a brush, coat the paprika-sprinkled side of each drumstick with the yogurt mixture. Turn the drumsticks over, sieve another tablespoon of paprika over them, and coat them with the remaining yogurt mixture. Set the drumsticks aside for 3 hours, until the yogurt begins to dry.

Lightly oil the barbecue rack. Cook the drumsticks over hot coals for 15 to 20 minutes, turning them every 5 minutes. After the last turn, sprinkle the remaining paprika over the drumsticks. Serve the drumsticks immediately, garnished with crisp salad leaves.

Poussins with Rum

Serves 4

Working time: about 30 minutes

Total time: about 1 hour and 20 minutes (includes marinating)

Calories 190

Protein 27g

Cholesterol 90mg

Total fat 4g

Saturated fat 1g

Sodium 120mg

2	small poussins (about 350 g/12 oz each)	2
1½ tbsp	clear honey garlic clove, crushed	1½ tbsp
2 tbsp	dark rum lime, juice only	2 tbsp
⅛ tsp	salt	⅛ tsp
1 tbsp	coriander seeds	1 tbsp
2 tsp	black peppercorns	2 tsp

Using either a pair of poultry shears or strong kitchen scissors, halve each poussin lengthwise by cutting through the backbone and breastbone. Cut off and discard the leg tips and the parson's nose. Wash the poussin halves under running water and pat them dry.

In a small bowl, mix together the rum, lime juice, honey, garlic and salt. Place the poussin halves in a shallow dish just large enough to accommodate them. Rub the rum mixture all over the poussins, then set them aside in a cool place, covered, and leave them to marinate for 30 minutes.

Using either a mortar and pestle or a coffee grinder, coarsely crush the coriander seeds and

the black peppercorns. Remove the poussin halves from the marinade and reserve the marinade. Thread two of the poussin halves on to each of two long metal skewers, piercing the legs and wings. Brush the skewered poussins with a little of the remaining rum marinade, then press the crushed coriander seeds and peppercorns all over the skin side of the birds.

Lightly oil the barbecue rack. Cook the poussins over hot coals for 20 to 25 minutes, turning the birds every 5 minutes, until the juices run clear when a skewer is inserted into a thigh.

Spit-Roasted Savoury Chicken

<table>
<tr><td>Serves 8</td></tr>
<tr><td>Working time: about 35 minutes</td></tr>
<tr><td>Total time: about 7 hours (includes marinating)</td></tr>
</table>

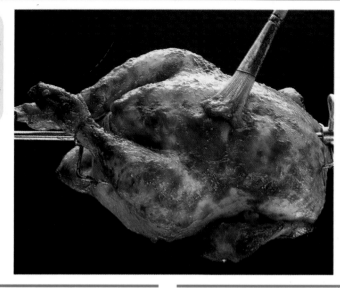

<table>
<tr><td>Calories
195</td></tr>
<tr><td>Protein
24g</td></tr>
<tr><td>Cholesterol
90mg</td></tr>
<tr><td>Total fat
9g</td></tr>
<tr><td>Saturated fat
2g</td></tr>
<tr><td>Sodium
85mg</td></tr>
</table>

2 tbsp	safflower oil	**2 tbsp**
1	small onion, grated	**1**
500 g	tomatoes, skinned, seeded, and chopped	**1 lb**
½	lemon, strained juice only	**½**

2 tbsp	Worcester sauce	**2 tbsp**
1 tsp	Tabasco sauce	**1 tsp**
1 tsp	dry mustard	**1 tsp**
2 tbsp	dark brown sugar	**2 tbsp**
1.75 kg	roasting chicken	**3 ½ lb**

Heat the oil in a heavy saucepan over low heat. Add the onion and cook for 2 minutes, until it is softened but not browned. Stir in the tomatoes, lemon juice, Worcester sauce, Tabasco sauce, mustard and sugar. Cover the pan and simmer the ingredients for 15 minutes, stirring occasionally, until the tomatoes are reduced to a purée. Remove the pan from the heat and pour the marinade into a bowl, then set it aside until it is cool—about 1 hour.

Put the chicken in a large bowl and pour the cooled marinade over it. Cover the bowl and leave the chicken to marinate for at least 4 hours, at room temperature, turning it several times.

Push a barbecue spit rod into the marinated chicken through the neck flap just above the breast bone, and out just above the tail. Secure the spit rod with the holding forks and attach the spit to the barbecue, on the turning mechanism. Rearrange the coals to leave room for a drip tray immediately below the chicken; set the drip tray in place.

Cook the chicken for 1¼ to 1½ hours, or until it is tender and the juices run clear when a thigh is pierced with a skewer. Baste the chicken frequently while it is cooking, first with the marinade, then with the cooking juices from the drip tray.

Bitter-Sweet Duck Breast Salad

Serves 6

Working time:
about 30
minutes

Total time:
about 8 hours
and 30
minutes
(includes
marinating)

Calories
145
Protein
14g
Cholesterol
75mg
Total fat
9g
Saturated fat
2g
Sodium
215mg

4	dried bay leaves	**4**
½ tsp	salt	**½ tsp**
12	juniper berries	**12**
1 tsp	mixed peppercorns	**1 tsp**
2 tsp	coriander seeds	**2 tsp**
500 g	duck breast fillets, skinned	**1 lb**
250 g	chicory, separated into leaves, washed and dried	**8 oz**
4 tsp	virgin olive oil	**4 tsp**
100 g	watercress, washed, dried	**3½ oz**
2	small oranges, rind finely shredded, fruit segmented	**2**
15 g	shelled walnuts	**½ oz**
2 tsp	walnut oil	**2 tsp**
2½ tbsp	fresh orange juice	**2½ tbsp**

Pound the bay leaves to a powder with the salt. Add the juniper berries, peppercorns and coriander seeds, and crush to a fine powder. Rub over the duck breasts, then place them in a dish. Cover and marinate the duck in the refrigerator for at least 8 hours.

Remove the duck from the refrigerator at least 1 hour before cooking. Wipe the meat with paper towels. Brush with 1 teaspoon of the olive oil, and lightly oil the barbecue rack.

Put the chicory, watercress, orange segments and walnuts in a salad bowl. Mix the walnut oil with 2 tsps of the olive oil and 1½ tbsp of the orange juice. Set aside.

Mix the remaining olive oil and orange juice, and brush a little over the duck breasts. Cook the duck over medium-hot coals for 2 minutes, then turn the breasts and cook them 3 to 4 minutes more, until the meat is lightly browned on the outside but still slightly pink in the middle. Turn the breasts now and then during cooking, brushing them with the juice and oil mixture.

Rest the cooked duck to rest for 2 to 3 minutes, then slice into strips and add to the chicory and watercress. Add the orange rind. Remix the dressing, pour it over the salad and toss.

Mustard-Marinated Rabbit with Brandied Peaches

Serves 6

Working time: about 35 minutes

Total time: about 7 hours (includes marinating)

Calories 470

Protein 24g

Cholesterol 25g

Total fat 10g

Saturated fat 4g

Sodium 35mg

2	garlic cloves, crushed	2
1 kg	rabbit, jointed in six portions, trimmed of fat and membrane	2 lb
6	juniper berries	6
30 cl	red wine	$\frac{1}{2}$ pint
1 tbsp	virgin olive oil	1 tbsp
1 tbsp	grainy mustard	1 tbsp
1 tsp	light brown sugar	1 tsp
2 tbsp	soured cream	2 tbsp

	Spiced brandied peaches	
175 g	light brown sugar	6 oz
30 cl	brandy	$\frac{1}{2}$ pint
30 cl	fruity white wine	$\frac{1}{2}$ pint
$\frac{1}{2}$	large lemon, juice and pared rind	$\frac{1}{2}$
2 tbsp	ground mixed spice	2 tbsp
1	cinnamon stick	1
1 tsp	grated nutmeg	1 tsp
6	firm peaches, halved and stoned	6

Smear the garlic over the rabbit pieces and place them in a dish. Toast the juniper berries in a heavy frying pan over high heat until they release their aroma—about 2 minutes. Add them to the wine with the oil, mustard, sugar and cream, and whisk together with a fork. Pour over the rabbit and marinate the meat for 6 to 8 hours, turning it every hour.

About an hour before you cook the rabbit, place the sugar, brandy, wine, lemon juice and rind, mixed spice, cinnamon and nutmeg in a pan just large enough to take the 12 peach halves. Bring to the boil and add the peaches, skin side down. Reduce the heat, cover, and simmer the peaches gently for 15 minutes, turning them once. Set aside.

Remove the rabbit pieces from their dish and reserve the marinade. Cook the rabbit joints over hot coals for 25 to 30 minutes, turning several times and basting with marinade.

Use a slotted spoon to remove the peaches from their pan. Place two, skin side down, on each of six serving plates. Strain the syrup and pour 1 tbsp over each peach half. Serve with the rabbit.

Pork Sheftalias with Oregano

Serves 6

Working time:
about 25
minutes

Total time:
about 4 hours
and 45 minutes
(includes
marinating)

Calories
190

Protein
25g

Cholesterol
55mg

Total fat
5g

Saturated fat
2g

Sodium
220mg

500 g	lean pork, trimmed of fat and minced	**1 lb**	
1	large onion	**1**	
4 tsp	chopped fresh oregano, or 1 tsp dried oregano	**4 tsp**	

2 tbsp	chopped flat-leaf parsley	**2 tbsp**	
3 tbsp	red wine	**3 tbsp**	
	freshly ground black pepper		
90 g	fresh breadcrumbs	**3 oz**	
¼ tsp	salt	**¼ tsp**	

Put the pork in a bowl and coarsely grate the onion over it. Mix in the oregano, parsley, wine and plenty of pepper. Cover the bowl and put the meat in the refrigerator to marinate for at least 4 hours, or overnight.

Add the breadcrumbs and salt to the marinated pork and mix them in well. In a separate bowl, whisk the egg white until it is fluffy but not stiff, then fold it into the pork and breadcrumb mixture. Shape the mixture into 18 balls. Cut the caul into 18 pieces, each about 12 cm (5 inches) in diameter. Loosely

wrap a piece of caul round each ball. Lightly oil the barbecue rack, and cook the sheftalias over hot coals for about 20 minutes, or until they are cooked inside and firm but slightly spongy when pressed; turn the pork balls every 3 to 4 minutes during cooking.

Editor's Note: Caul is a weblike fatty membrane that surrounds a pig's stomach. It is available from butchers either fresh or dry-salted. If the latter, rinse before use.

Piquant Pork Chops

1	lime, juice only	**1**	**1 tsp**	allspice	**1 tsp**
2 tsp	honey	**2 tsp**		freshly ground black pepper	
1 tsp	Tabasco sauce	**1 tsp**	**4**	pork loin chops	**4**
1 tbsp	red wine vinegar	**1 tbsp**		(about 175 g/6 oz each),	
75 g	unsalted tomato paste	**2 ½ oz**		trimmed of fat	

Mix the lime juice, honey, Tabasco sauce, vinegar, tomato paste, allspice and some freshly ground black pepper together in a large bowl. Add the pork chops, and turn them so that they are evenly coated with the marinade. Place the chops in the refrigerator and leave them to marinate for 8 hours, or overnight. Remove them from the refrigerator about an hour before you plan to cook them.

Lightly oil the barbecue rack, and cook the pork chops over hot coals for about 6 minutes on each side, basting them with any remaining marinade.

Skewers of Spiced Pork, Aubergine and Pepper

Serves 12

Working time:
about 30 minutes

Total time:
about 2 hours and 30 minutes
(includes marinating)

Calories
155
Protein
22g
Cholesterol
50mg
Total fat
6g
Saturated fat
2g
Sodium
100mg

1 kg	lean pork fillets, trimmed of all fat cut into 1 cm (½ inch) medallions	**2 lb**
3	aubergines, cut into 2.5cm (1 inch) thick slices and quartered	**3**
3	sweet green peppers, seeded, deribbed and cut into 2.5 cm (1 inch) squares	**3**
1 tbsp	safflower oil	**1 tbsp**
	Garlic and cumin marinade	
2	green chili peppers, seeded and finely chopped	**2**
1	small onion, thinly sliced	**1**

2.5 cm	piece fresh ginger root, finely chopped	**1 inch**
4	garlic cloves, crushed	**4**
3	bay leaves	**3**
1	lime, grated rind and juice	**1**
2	cinnamon sticks, halved	**2**
1 tbsp	whole cloves	**1 tbsp**
2 tsp	ground cumin	**2 tsp**
¼ tsp	ground turmeric	**¼ tsp**
1 tbsp	garam masala	**1 tbsp**
½ tsp	salt	**½ tsp**
	freshly ground black pepper	
15 cl	low-fat yogurt	**¼ pint**

In a bowl, mix together the marinade ingredients. Add the pork medallions, tossing them in the marinade to coat them well. Cover the bowl and chill the meat in the refrigerator for 2 to 4 hours.

Remove the pork medallions from the marinade and discard the bay leaves, cloves and pieces of cinnamon stick. Thread the pork on to 12 skewers, pushing the skewers through the circumference of each medallion. Thread the pieces of aubergine and sweet green pepper alternately on to 12 more skewers. Brush the vegetable kebabs with the safflower oil.

Oil the barbecue lightly and cook the kebabs over hot coals for 3 to 4 minutes on each side, until the meat is lightly browned and cooked through and the vegetables are tender. Serve immediately.

Pork and Apple Kebabs

Serves 4

Working time:
about 45
minutes

Total time:
about 2 hours
and 45
minutes
(includes
marinating)

Calories
300
Protein
35g
Cholesterol
80mg
Total fat
12g
Saturated fat
4g
Sodium
100mg

30 cl	dry cider	**½ pint**	
6	black peppercorns, crushed	**6**	
½ tsp	ground cloves	**½ tsp**	
2 tsp	finely chopped fresh sage	**2 tsp**	
2 tsp	chopped fresh rosemary	**2 tsp**	
500 g	pork tender loin, trimmed of fat, cut in to 2.5 cm (1 inch) cubes	**1 lb**	
1 tbsp	safflower oil	**1 tbsp**	
2	crisp dessert apples	**2**	

Pour the cider into a large bowl. Add the peppercorns, cloves, sage and rosemary, and stir well. Add the pork cubes to the bowl, turning them to coat them evenly. Cover the pork, and set it aside to marinate for at least 2 hours at room temperature.

Remove the cubes of pork from the marinade and reserve the marinade. Lightly oil four skewers. Core the apples and cut each one into six wedges; dip each piece of apple in the reserved marinade. Thread pieces of pork and apple alternately on to each of the four skewers, starting and ending with a cube of pork. Stir the oil into the remaining marinade and baste the kebabs with this mixture.

Place the kebabs on the barbecue rack and cook them, over hot coals, for 15 to 20 minutes, until they are cooked through; turn the kebabs and baste them with marinade several times during cooking.

Lamb Noisettes with Tomato and Olive Relish

Serves 4

Working time:
about 30
minutes

Total time:
about 5 hours
and 30
minutes
(includes
marinating)

Calories
225
Protein
28g
Cholesterol
70mg
Total fat
10g
Saturated fat
4g
Sodium
180mg

4	long thick rosemary twigs	4
4	lean large noisettes of lamb (about 100 g/3 $\frac{1}{2}$ oz each), trimmed of fat	4
1	onion, thinly sliced	1
2	garlic cloves, chopped	2
1 tsp	chopped fresh oregano, or $\frac{1}{4}$ tsp dried oregano	1 tsp
$\frac{1}{4}$ tsp	salt	$\frac{1}{4}$ tsp
	freshly ground black pepper	
15 cl	medium white wine	$\frac{1}{4}$ pint

Tomato and olive relish

1 tsp	virgin olive oil	1 tsp
1	small onion, finely chopped	1
8	black olives, stoned and finely chopped	8
2 tsp	white wine vinegar	2 tsp
$\frac{1}{2}$ tsp	caster sugar	$\frac{1}{2}$ tsp
2 tsp	chopped fresh thyme, or $\frac{1}{2}$ tsp dried thyme	2 tsp
2 tbsp	medium white wine, or water	2 tbsp
5	tomatoes, skinned, seeded, coarsely chopped and drained	5

Push a rosemary twig through each noisette, then place in a shallow dish in a single layer. Sprinkle the onion, garlic, oregano, salt and some pepper evenly over the lamb, then pour on the wine. Cover, for about 4 hours; turn the noisettes several times during this period. Remove from the refrigerator about 1 hour before cooking.

For the relish, heat the oil in a small saucepan. Add the onion and cook it very gently for about 8 minutes, stirring occasionally, until softened. Stir in the olives, vinegar, sugar, thyme, wine and tomatoes. Remove from the heat and set aside.

Lightly oil the barbecue rack, and cook the noisettes over hot coals for 6 to 8 minutes per side, are firm and browned. Meanwhile, reheat the relish and transfer it to a small bowl. Remove the strings from the noisettes and serve them accompanied by the relish.

Lamb Burgers with Basil and Parmesan Sauce

750 g	lean leg of lamb, trimmed of fat, minced	**1½ lb**			freshly ground black pepper	
				½ tsp	virgin olive oil	**½ tsp**
3	onions, chopped	**3**		**15 cl**	unsalted vegetable stock	**¼ pint**
250 g	courgettes, coarsely grated	**8 oz**		**15 g**	basil leaves, roughly chopped	**½ oz**
90 g	fresh wholemeal breadcrumbs	**3 oz**		**30 g**	Parmesan cheese; freshly grated	**1 oz**
¼ tsp	salt	**¼ tsp**				

Put the minced lamb in a bowl. Add a third of the chopped onions, the courgettes, breadcrumbs, salt and some freshly ground black pepper. Using a wooden spoon or your hands, work the ingredients together until they are thoroughly combined. Divide the mixture into 16 equal portions, then shape each portion into a burger about 6 cm (2 ½ inches) in diameter and 1 cm (½ inch) thick. Place the burgers on a baking sheet and set them aside.

Heat the oil in a small saucepan over medium heat. Add the remaining chopped onions and cook them gently for about 3 minutes, until they are beginning to soften.

Pour the stock into the pan and bring it to the boil, then cover the pan and reduce the heat. Simmer the liquid for 4 to 5 minutes, until the onion is tender. Stir in the basil and cheese, and season the sauce with some pepper. Cook the sauce for a further minute, then transfer it to a food processor or blender and process it until it is smooth. Pour the sauce back into the saucepan, and set it aside ready to be reheated very gently just before serving.

Lightly oil the barbecue rack, and cook the burgers over hot coals for 7 to 8 minutes on each side. Serve them at once, with the reheated sauce.

Lamb Skewers with Plantain

Serves 4

Working time:
about 30
minutes

Total time
about 1 hour

Calories
425

Protein
31g

Cholesterol
80mg

Total fat
16g

Saturated fat
5g

Sodium
160mg

500g	lean lamb (from the eye of loin or fillet), trimmed of fat	1 lb	1	garlic clove, finely chopped	1
1 tbsp	virgin olive oil	1 tbsp	¼ tsp	salt	¼ tsp
3 drops	Angostura bitters	3 drops		freshly ground black pepper	
1 tsp	coarsely chopped fresh thyme leaves	1 tsp	2	ripe plantains (325g/11 oz each)	2

Cut the trimmed lamb into disc-shaped slices about 1 cm (½ inch) thick. Squeeze each disc of lamb into a crescent shape and skewer it lengthwise so that the skewer maintains the crescent form; divide the crescents among four skewers. Place the skewers on a tray or a large, flat plate and set them aside.

In a small bowl, combine the olive oil, Angostura bitters, chopped garlic and thyme, salt and some freshly ground black pepper. Brush the lamb skewers with this marinade and leave them, covered, in a cool place for 30 minutes, or up to 3 hours.

Meanwhile, prepare the plantain skewers. Top and tail the plantains, and place them in a large saucepan of boiling water Boil the plantains, uncovered, for 20 minutes, then drain them and allow them to cool. When they are cool enough to handle, peel them and cut each one lengthwise into four slices. Cut each slice of plantain into 5 cm (2 inch) long pieces. Fold over each piece of plantain so that its ends almost meet, and thread the slices on to four skewers. Brush the plantain skewers lightly with oil.

Place the lamb and the plantain skewers on the barbecue rack over hot coals and cook them for 6 minutes, turning them once as they cook.

Spit-Roasted Moroccan Lamb

Serves 12

Working time: about 30 minutes

Total time: about 6 hours and 30 minutes (includes marinating)

Calories 275

Protein 37g

Cholesterol 100mg

Total fat 14g

Saturated fat 5g

Sodium 85mg

2 kg	lean leg of lamb, skin and all visible fat removed	**4 lb**
4	garlic cloves, each cut lengthwise into eight slivers	**4**
3 tbsp	safflower oil	**3 tbsp**

1 tbsp	ground cumin	**1 tbsp**
2 tbsp	ground coriander	**2 tbsp**
2 tsp	ground cinnamon	**2 tsp**
2 tbsp	chopped mint	**2 tbsp**

Discard the knuckle from the leg of lamb. Make deep incisions about 5 cm (2 inches) apart all over the joint, and insert the garlic slivers into the cuts. Place the joint in a large dish. Mix together the oil, cumin, coriander, cinnamon and mint, and rub half of the mixture over the lamb, coating it completely. Set the remaining spice and mint mixture aside. Cover the meat and leave it to marinate in the refrigerator for at least 4 hours, or overnight. Remove the meat from the refrigerator about 2 hours before you plan to

cook it, to allow it to reach room temperature.

Fix the joint diagonally on to a rotating spit so that the weight is evenly distributed and the spit will turn easily. Roast the meat, rotating it, over very hot coals. Start carving slices from the lamb after 15 to 20 minutes, leaving the rest of the joint on the spit to continue cooking. Baste the area from which you have carved the slices with the reserved spice and mint marinade. Continue to carve slices from the lamb about every 10 minutes as it cooks.

Barbecued Escalope of Veal

Serves 4

Working time: about 25 minutes

Total time: about 4 hours and 25 minutes (includes marinating)

Calories 150
Protein 53g
Cholesterol 30mg
Total fat 7g
Saturated fat 5g
Sodium 220mg

8	small thin-cut veal escalopes (about 45g/1½ oz each), trimmed of fat	**8**
4 tbsp	plain low-fat yogurt	**4 tbsp**
1 tbsp	virgin olive oil	**1 tbsp**
1 tbsp	balsamic vinegar	**1 tbsp**
1 tbsp	grainy mustard	**1 tbsp**
	white pepper	
8	fresh sage leaves, finely chopped	**8**
¼ tsp	salt	**¼ tsp**
	coarsely crushed white peppercorns (optional)	

Lay an escalope on the work surface between two sheets of plastic film. Using the smooth side of a meat-bat or a rolling pin, pound the meat until it is about 1.5 mm. Repeat this process with the other escalopes. In a small bowl, whisk together the yogurt, oil, vinegar, mustard, pepper and chopped sage leaves. Brush the escalopes with the marinade and place them in a shallow dish; reserve any remaining marinade. Cover the dish, and leave the escalopes to marinate for 4 to 6 hours at room temperature, or for 12 to 24 hours in the refrigerator. The escalopes should be removed from the refrigerator about 1 hour before you plan to cook them.

Cook the escalopes over hot coals for 45 seconds on each side, basting them with any remaining marinade. Sprinkle the cooked escalopes with the salt and, if you like, with crushed white peppercorns. Serve the escalopes immediately.

Mustard Steaks with Yogurt Sauce Served with Salad

Serves 4

Working time:
about 20
minutes

Total time:
about 45
minutes

Calories
325
Protein
45g
Cholesterol
100mg
Total fat
14g
Saturated fat
6g
Sodium
125mg

4	sirloin steaks (about 150g/5 oz each), trimmed of fat	4
2 tbsp	grainy mustard, tarragon flavoured if possible	2 tbsp
2	garlic cloves, crushed	2
15 cl	plain low-fat yogurt	$\frac{1}{4}$ pint
	freshly ground black pepper	

Chicory salad

90 g	button mushrooms, wiped and trimmed	3 oz
2 tbsp	fresh lemon juice	2 tbsp
175 g	chicory, trimmed and thinly sliced	6 oz
1	box mustard and cress	1
4	spring onions, trimmed and sliced	4
$\frac{1}{2}$	sweet orange or red pepper, sliced and blanched	$\frac{1}{2}$

Starting at the untrimmed side of each steak, cut a pocket almost through to the opposite side. Coat the insides of the pockets with half of the mustard, then rub the steaks all over with half of the crushed garlic. Put the steaks in a dish and set them aside in a cool place, covered, to marinate for 30 minutes.

Meanwhile, make the yogurt sauce. Put the yogurt, the remaining mustard and garlic, and plenty of black pepper in a bowl, and mix them together thoroughly.

For the salad, slice the mushrooms and put them in a bowl with the lemon juice. Toss the mushrooms well and leave them to stand for 10 minutes. Add the chicory, mustard and cress, spring onions and sweet pepper, and mix them together well. Cover the salad and chill it until required.

Brush the barbecue rack with oil and cook the mustard steaks over hot coals for 3 to 5 minutes on each side. Serve the steaks with the salad and sauce.

Steakburgers with Parsnips and Brown Ale

Serves 12

Working (and total) time about 50 minutes

Calories 130
Protein 17g
Cholesterol 35mg
Total fat 5g
Saturated fat 2g
Sodium 125mg

20 cl	strong brown ale	7 fl oz
750 g	lean steak, trimmed of fat and minced	1½ lb
1	onion, finely chopped	1
300 g	parsnips, peeled and finely grated	10 oz

2 tsp	chopped fresh thyme	2 tsp
2 tbsp	chopped parsley	2 tbsp
45 g	fresh wholemeal breadcrumbs	1½oz
1 tbsp	grainy mustard	1 tbsp
½ tsp	salt	½ tsp
	freshly ground black pepper	

In a small, heavy-bottomed pan, bring the ale to the boil, then reduce the heat and boil gently until it has reduced to 4 tablespoons—about 5 minutes. Put the steak in a large bowl and add the onion, parsnips, thyme, parsley, breadcrumbs, mustard, salt and some pepper. Pour in the ale. Using a wooden spoon, work the mixture together to combine the ingredients.

Divide the mixture into 12 equal portions. Shape each portion into a ball between your palms, then flatten the balls into burger shapes on a chopping board. Lightly oil the barbecue rack and cook the steakburgers over medium-hot coals for 7 to 8 minutes on each side, until they are just cooked through.

Shoulder of Lamb with Anchovy Stuffing

Serves 10

Working time:
about 45
minutes

Total time:
about 12
hours
(includes
marinating)

Calories
185
Protein
24g
Cholesterol
65mg
Total fat
9g
Saturated fat
3g
Sodium
290mg

15 g	fresh rosemary	**½ oz**
15 g	parsley	**½ oz**
3	garlic cloves	**3**
½	lemon, grated rind and juice	**½**
60 g	canned anchovy fillets in oil	**2 oz**
	freshly ground black pepper	
1 kg	shoulder of lamb, skinned boned and trimmed	**2½ lb**

	Lemon sauce	
1 tbsp	virgin olive oil	**1 tbsp**
1	small onion, finely chopped	**1**
1 tbsp	plain flour	**1 tbsp**
45 cl	unsalted chicken stock	**½ pint**
1	lemon, grated rind and juice	**1**
2 tbsp	chopped parsley	**2 tbsp**

Place the rosemary in a food processor with the parsley, garlic, lemon rind and juice, anchovies with their oil, and some black pepper. Process to a smooth paste.

Wipe the lamb. Lay it out flat, boned side uppermost, and spread on the paste. Fold the two opposite sides of the meat over the filling to meet in the centre; secure with metal skewers. Cover marinate in the refrigerator for at least 8 hours. Remove from the refrigerator about 2 hours before cooking.

Lightly oil the barbecue rack, and cook the lamb over medium-hot coals for about 2 hours, turning frequently. The juices should then run clear when the lamb is pierced.

About 20 minutes before the lamb is ready, heat the oil in a small, heavy saucepan. Add the onion and cook until transparent. Stir in the flour and cook for 1 minute, stirring. Gradually pour in the stock, stirring continuously, and bring to the boil. Simmer the sauce for 10 minutes, then stir in the lemon rind and juice, and simmer for 5 minutes more. Remove the pan from the heat. Stir in the parsley into the sauce just before you serve it.

Serve the lamb sliced, with the sauce.

Tabbouleh

Serves 6

Working time:
about 30
minutes

Total time:
about 1 hour
(includes
soaking)

Calories
75

Protein
3g

Cholesterol
0mg

Total fat
3g

Saturated fat
1g

Sodium
10mg

90 g	burghul	**3 oz**
20 g	mint leaves, finely chopped	**¾ oz**
60 g	parsley, finely chopped	**2 oz**
1	onion, finely chopped	**1**

3 tbsp	fresh lemon juice	**3 tbsp**
1 tbsp	virgin olive oil	**1 tbsp**
	tomato wedges, for garnish	

Put the burghul in a bowl and add sufficient boiling water to cover it. Leave the burghul to soak for 30 minutes, topping up the water as necessary to keep the grains covered. Tip the burghul into a nylon sieve and let it drain thoroughly; press it down with the back of a spoon to force out as much moisture as possible.

Turn the drained burghul into a mixing bowl and add the mint, parsley, onion, lemon juice and oil. Stir all the ingredients together thoroughly. Place the tabbouleh in a lidded plastic container, and place it in the refrigerator until required. Chill the tomato wedges in a separate container.

To serve, transfer the tabbouleh to a serving bowl and garnish it with the tomato wedges.

Carrots Cooked with Honey and Spices

Serves 6

Working time:
about 5
minutes

Total time:
about 15
minutes

Calories
35
Protein
1g
Cholesterol
0mg
Total fat
0g
Saturated fat
0g
Sodium
210mg

500g	carrots, sliced diagonally	**1 lb**
	small onion, finely chopped	
2 tbsp	clear honey	**2 tbsp**
2 tbsp	wine vinegar	**2 tbsp**

1 tsp	ground cumin	**1 tsp**
½ tsp	ground cinnamon	**½ tsp**
2 tsp	salt	**2 tsp**
2 tbsp	chopped parsley	**2 tbsp**

Place the carrots, onion, honey, wine vinegar, cumin, cinnamon and salt in a heavy-bottomed saucepan, and add 15 cl (¼ pint) of water. Set the pan over high heat and bring the liquid to the boil. Reduce the heat a little, and cook the carrots fairly rapidly, uncovered, for about 10 minutes, until most of the liquid has evaporated but the carrots are still slightly crunchy. Set the mixture aside to cool.

Transfer the carrots to a lidded container, then chill them in the refrigerator required.

To serve, turn the carrots into a serving bowl and sprinkle on the chopped parsley.

Mushroom and Parsley Pâté

Serves 6

Working time: about 25 minutes

Total time: about 24 hours (includes chilling)

Calories 85
Protein 4g
Cholesterol 0mg
Total fat 3g
Saturated fat 1g
Sodium 205mg

1 tbsp	polyunsaturated margarine	1 tbsp
2	garlic cloves, crushed	2
1	large onion, finely chopped	1
625 g	flat mushrooms, wiped and roughly chopped	1¼ oz
20 g	flat-leaf parsley, chopped	¾ oz

	freshly ground black pepper	
1 tbsp	mango chutney, chopped	1 tbsp
2 tbsp	white wine vinegar	2 tbsp
¼ tsp	salt	¼ tsp
90 g	fresh wholemeal breadcrumbs	3 oz

Place the margarine in a large bowl and microwave it on high for 30 seconds, or until it has melted. Stir the garlic and onion thoroughly into the margarine, and cook them on high for 2 minutes.

Stir in the mushrooms, and cook the mixture on high for another 5 minutes. Add half the chopped parsley and some black pepper, mix them in, and cook on high for a further 5 minutes. Stir the chopped mango chutney, wine vinegar and salt into the mushroom mixture, making sure that all the ingredients are thoroughly combined. Cook on high for 5 minutes more, or until all the liquid has evaporated. Mix in the breadcrumbs and the remaining chopped parsley.

Spoon the pâté into a round dish about 15 cm (6 inches) in diameter and 7.5 cm (3 inches) in depth. Press the mixture down lightly with the back of the spoon. Leave the pâté to cool and then chill for about 24 hours to allow the flavours to develop fully.

Garlic Potato Fans and Grilled Corn-on-the-Cob

Serves 12

Working time: about 30 minutes

Total time: about 2 hours and 30 minutes

Calories 385

Protein 9g

Cholesterol 0mg

Total fat 8g

Saturated fat 1g

Sodium 15mg

1	large garlic clove, lightly crushed	1
4 tbsp	corn or safflower oil	**4 tbsp**
12	ears sweetcorn in the husk	12

| 12 | baking potatoes (250g/8oz each), scrubbed | 12 |

At least 1 hour before you begin to cook the potatoes, combine the garlic and oil in a cup. Set them aside to allow the garlic to infuse the oil.

Make crosswise cuts about 1 cm ($\frac{1}{2}$ inch) apart in the baking potatoes, cutting about two thirds of the way through. Place each potato on a double-thickness square of foil that is large enough to wrap round it. Brush the garlic-flavoured oil over the potatoes so that it can seep down into the cuts. Wrap the foil square securely round the potatoes.

Place the foil parcels on the barbecue rack, over hot coals. Roast the potatoes for about 1 hour, turning them occasionally so that they cook evenly.

To prepare the corn-on-the-cob, fold back the husks on each ear and remove the silk. Fold the husks back up round the corn, then wrap each ear securely in a double thickness of foil. Place the foil-wrapped corn on the barbecue rack and cook it for 15 to 20 minutes, turning it occasionally so that it cooks evenly.

To serve, remove the foil from the corn cobs, then very carefully peel back and trim off one side of the husks: the corn inside will be extremely hot. Open out the foil round the potatoes and pinch their sides to open up the cuts. Pile the vegetables on platters.

Fruited Cabbage Salad

Serves 12

Working time:
about 25
minutes

Total time:
about 1 hour

Calories
105
Protein
4g
Cholesterol
trace
Total fat
3g
Saturated fat
1g
Sodium
45mg

350g	trimmed red cabbage, finely shredded	**12 oz**
350g	trimmed white cabbage, finely shredded	**12 oz**
250 g	trimmed Chinese cabbage, finely shredded	**8 oz**
1	red onion, cut into fine slivers	**1**
250 g	seedless green grapes, halved if large	**8 oz**
1 tbsp	caraway seeds	**1 tbsp**
2	dessert apples, cored, diced, sprinkled with fresh lemon juice	**2**
	Honey dressing	
8 cl	cider vinegar	**3 fl oz**
3 tbsp	Greek honey, or other clear honey	**3 tbsp**
1 tbsp	Dijon mustard	**1 tbsp**
2 tbsp	corn or safflower oil	**2 tbsp**
¼ litre	plain low-fat yogurt	**8 fl oz**
	freshly ground black pepper	

First make the dressing. In a small bowl, combine the vinegar, honey and mustard, and whisk them together. Gradually whisk in the corn oil, followed by the yogurt. Season the dressing with some black pepper.

In a large mixing bowl, combine the red, white and Chinese cabbages, the onion, grapes and apples. Pour the dressing over the salad, and sprinkle on the caraway seeds. Lift and toss the salad until the fruit and vegetables are evenly coated with the dressing.

Cover the bowl and chill the salad for at least 30 minutes before serving it. Stir and toss the salad again before transferring it to a serving dish.

Salad of Lettuce and Nasturtium Flowers

Serves 6

Working (and total) time: about 20 minutes

Calories
25
Protein
1g
Cholesterol
10mg
Total fat
2g
Saturated fat
1g
Sodium
75mg

1	small cos lettuce, or two little gem lettuces, leaves washed and dried	**1**
1	red lollo lettuce, leaves washed and dried	**1**
12	nasturtium flowers	**12**

	Mustard-lemon dressing	
4 tbsp	soured cream	**4 tbsp**
2 tbsp	fresh lemon juice	**2 tbsp**
2 tsp	Dijon mustard	**2 tsp**
¼ tsp	salt	**¼ tsp**
	freshly ground black pepper	
2 tbsp	finely cut chives	**2 tbsp**

To make the dressing, put all the ingredients into a screw-top jar and shake them together vigorously. Chill the dressing until it is required.

Before serving, shake the dressing again, then pour it into the bottom of a serving bowl. Tear the lettuce leaves into pieces and place in the bowl. Arrange the flowers on top. Just before serving, toss the salad with the dressing.

Pork Rolls with Fennel

Serves 4

Working time:
about 1 hour
and 30
minutes

Total time:
about 10
hours
(includes
marinating)

Calories
310
Protein
38g
Cholesterol
85mg
Total fat
16g
Saturated fat
4g
Sodium
150mg

2	pork fillets (275 g/9 oz each)	**2**
2 tbsp	virgin olive oil	**2 tbsp**
1 tsp	fennel seeds, crushed	**1 tsp**
1	garlic clove, crushed	**1**
2	lemons, finely grated rind and juice freshly ground black pepper	**2**

1	fennel bulb (about 250 g/8 oz), finely chopped, leaves reserved	**1**
⅛ tsp	salt	**⅛ tsp**
1 tsp	clear honey	**1 tsp**

Cut down the length of each fillet, three quarters of the way through. Open out each fillet and lay it flat on a plastic film; cover with more plastic film. Beat out the fillets into oblongs about 5 mm (¼ inch) thick. Lay in a large dish. Mix the oil with the fennel seeds, garlic, lemon rind and 4 tbsps of water. Add black pepper and the chopped fennel. Spread the mixture evenly over the pork, cover and marinate in the refrigerator for at least 6 hours.

Remove the pork from the dish, scrape the marinade into a bowl, and set the bowl aside. Lay the pork on a work surface and arrange the fennel leaves evenly over keeping a few for garnish. Sprinkle the chopped fennel

mixture with salt, then lift out the fennel and spread it over the pork; reserve the marinade. Roll up each fillet and tie with string. Wrap the rolls in double thickness foil parcels.

Place on the barbecue rack over hot coals and cook for 40 minutes, turning every 10 minutes. Remove the cooked pork from the foil, and transfer the cooking juices to a bowl. Stir in the lemon juice, honey and reserved marinade, then brush a little over each roll. Cook the pork without the foil, for a further 10 minutes, basting with the juices and turning until golden-brown. Cut each roll into four. Serve garnished with fennel leaves.

Chicken, Mango and Penne Salad

Serves 6

Working time: about 40 minutes

Total time: about 1 hour (includes cooling)

Calories 435

Protein 30g

Cholesterol 60mg

Total fat 8g

Saturated fat 5g

Sodium 160mg

4	skinned and boned chicken breasts, (about 500 g/1 lb)	**4**
2 tsp	low-sodium soy sauce or shoyu	**2 tsp**
350 g	penne (or other short, tubular pasta)	**12 oz**
250g	mange-tout, stems and strings removed	**8 oz**

2	large mangoes	**2**
	Coriander and coconut dressing	
17. 5 cl	plain low-fat yogurt	**6 fl oz**
1 tbsp	chopped fresh coriander	**1 tbsp**
¼ tsp	salt	**¼ tsp**
3 tbsp	freshly ground black pepper	**3 tbsp**

In a bowl, mix together all the ingredients for the yogurt dressing. Set the dressing aside.

Put the chicken breasts in a saucepan, and pour in 60 cl (1 pint) of water and the soy sauce; slowly bring the liquid to a simmer. Partially cover the saucepan, and poach the chicken breasts gently until the flesh is firm and opaque all the way through when pierced with the tip of a sharp knife—10 to 15 minutes. Remove the chicken breasts from the liquid with a slotted spoon, and set them aside to cool. When they are cold, carve them into slices.

While the chicken is cooling, bring ¾ litre

(6 pints) of water to the boil in a large saucepan. Add 2 teaspoons of salt and the penne. Start testing the pasta after 10 minutes, and cook it until it is *al dente*. Drain the pasta, refresh it under cold running water, and drain it again thoroughly. Blanch the mange-tout in a saucepan of boiling water, then refresh them under cold running water and drain them well. Peel the mangoes, and cut the flesh into slices.

Toss the chicken, penne and mange-tout in the yogurt dressing. Add the mango slices just before serving.

Minted Potato and Turkey Salad

Serves 4

Working time: about 30 minutes

Total time: about 40 minutes

Calories 275

Protein 21g

Cholesterol 40mg

Total fat 9g

Saturated fat 2g

Sodium 55mg

500 g	small new potatoes, scrubbed and cut into 1 cm (½ inch) chunks	**1lb**
2 tbsp	safflower oil	**2 tbsp**
2 tbsp	fresh lemon juice	**2 tbsp**
1 tbsp	white wine vinegar	**1 tbsp**
½	lemon, grated rind only	**½**
½ tsp	grainy mustard	**½ tsp**
1	garlic clove, crushed	**1**
⅛ tsp	salt	**⅛ tsp**
	freshly ground black pepper	
½ tsp	sugar	**½ tsp**
175 g	broccoli florets	**6 oz**
1	red-skinned dessert apple	**1**
300 g	cooked skinless turkey breast, cut into 1 cm (½ inch) cubes	**10 oz**
125 g	carrots, julienned	**4 oz**
3	spring onions, trimmed and sliced diagonally into 2.5 cm (1 inch) pieces	
	mint sprigs, for garnish	

Simmer the potatoes until they are tender but not too soft—about 10 minutes.

Meanwhile, whisk together the oil, 1 tablespoon of the lemon juice, the vinegar, lemon rind, mustard, garlic, salt, plenty of black pepper and the sugar.

Drain the potatoes and put them in a mixing bowl. Add the dressing and toss them well. Set the potatoes aside and leave them to cool.

Parboil the broccoli in a saucepan of boiling water for 1 to 2 minutes, then drain rinse under cold running water and drain again. Quarter and core the apple, cut it into thin slices and toss in the remaining lemon juice. Add the broccoli florets, apple, turkey, carrot sticks and spring onions to the potatoes. Toss together and transfer to a serving bowl. Put the mint sprigs into a plastic bag, and take a small pair of scissors to the picnic as well.

Cut one or two mint sprigs into strips over the salad. Finally, garnish the salad with a few whole mint sprigs.

Artichoke and Asparagus Salad

Serves 8 as a
side dish

Working time:
about 45
minutes

Total time:
about 1 hour

Calories
55
Protein
3g
Cholesterol
trace
Total fat
3g
Saturated fat
1g
Sodium
105mg

1	lemon, cut in half	1
4	globe artichokes	4
500 g	fine asparagus, trimmed	1 lb
1	red lollo lettuce, torn into large pieces	1
4	little gem lettuces, cut into chunks	4

Orange-hazelnut vinaigrette		
2 tbsp	fresh orange juice	2 tbsp
1 ½ tbsp	hazelnut oil	1 ½ tbsp
1 tsp	grainy mustard	1 tsp
½	orange, grated rind only	½
½ tsp	salt	½ tsp
	freshly ground black pepper	

Fill a large, saucepan with water. Squeeze one lemon half into the pan, then add the lemon half itself.

Remove enough outer leaves from each artichoke to expose the yellow-green inner leaves. Slice through about 4 cm (1 ½ inches) above the rounded base and discard the top. Cut off the stem flush with the end of the artichoke and rub the base with the the second lemon half. Pare off the bases of the leaves, then trim away the light green parts from the upper half of the artichoke, rubbing the cut surfaces with the lemon. Scrape out and discard the hairy choke from the centre. Drop the hearts into the pan of acidulated water.

Bring the pan to the boil and cook gently until tender—12 to 15 minutes. Refresh the hearts under cold running water, then cut each into 16.

While the artichokes are cooking, cook the asparagus in boiling water for 2 to 3 minutes. Refresh and drain it. Cut the spears diagonally into 2.5 cm (1 inch) pieces, keeping the tips intact.

Put the red lollo and little gem lettuce, the artichokes and the asparagus into a large salad bowl and chill. Put all the ingredients for the orange-hazelnut vinaigrette into a screw-topped jar and shake them together well.

Pour the dressing on to the salad and toss gently just before serving it.

Pear, Fennel and Watercress Salad

Serves 4

Working (and total) time: about 40 minutes

Calories
195
Protein
6g
Cholesterol
10mg
Total fat
11g
Saturated fat
3g
Sodium
305mg

75 g	light rye or other wholegrain bread, crusts removed, cut into 1 cm ($\frac{1}{2}$ inch) cubes	**2$\frac{1}{2}$ oz**
2	large ripe dessert pears cored, diced and placed in acidulated water	**2**
60 g	Edam cheese, cut into bâtonnets	**2 oz**
125 g	bulb fennel, trimmed and thinly sliced	**4 oz**

90 g	watercress, washed and dried, divided into sprigs	**3 oz**
	Lemon dressing	
$\frac{1}{4}$	thin-skinned lemon, roughly chopped	$\frac{1}{4}$
$\frac{1}{2}$ **tsp**	grainy mustard	$\frac{1}{2}$ **tsp**
1 tbsp	clear honey	**1 tbsp**
2 tbsp	virgin olive oil	**2 tbsp**

Preheat the oven to 180°C (350°F or Mark 4). Arrange the bread cubes on a baking sheet and toast them in the oven until they are golden-brown and crisp—about 20 minutes. Leave the croûtons to cool.

To prepare the dressing, put the chopped lemon, the mustard, honey and oil in a food processor or blender. Add 2 tablespoons of water and process the ingredients until they form a creamy purée.

Drain the diced pears and place them in a large mixing bowl, together with the cheese and fennel. Add the lemon dressing and toss the ingredients thoroughly.

Add the watercress and croûtons to the dressed salad, and toss all the ingredients together. Serve the salad at once.

Editor's Note: The pears, cheese and fennel can be prepared and dressed up to 12 hours in advance and stored.

Salad of Red Leaves, Beans and Roots

Serves 12 as a
side dish

Working time:
about 40
minutes

Total time:
about 3 hours

Calories
100

Protein
4g

Cholesterol
5mg

Total fat
6g

Saturated fat
2g

Sodium
75mg

175 g	dried red kidney beans, picked over	**6 oz**
250 g	red cabbage, finely shredded	**8 oz**
1	small red onion, quartered and finely sliced	**1**
300 g	raw beetroot, peeled and grated	**10 oz**
1	head radicchio, leaves washed and dried	**1**
30 g	blue Stilton cheese, crumbled	**1 oz**

1 tsp	poppy seeds	**1 tsp**
	Walnut vinaigrette	
1 tsp	grainy French mustard	**1 tsp**
⅛ tsp	Tabasco sauce	**⅛ tsp**
⅛ tsp	salt	**⅛ tsp**
⅛ tsp	freshly ground black pepper	**⅛ tsp**
2 tbsp	red wine vinegar	**2 tbsp**
4 tbsp	walnut oil	**4 tbsp**

Rinse the kidney beans under cold running water, then put them into a large saucepan well covered with cold water. Discard any beans that float to the surface. Cover the saucepan leaving the lid ajar, and slowly bring to the boil. Boil for two minutes, then turn off the heat and soak the beans, covered, for at least an hour.

Rinse the beans and place them in a clean saucepan with enough cold water to cover them by about 7.5 cm (3 inches). Boil them for 10 minutes, then rinse them and discard the water. Wash out the pan, replace the beans

and cover them with water as before, then simmer them until tender—about 1 hour. When they are cooked, drain and rinse the beans, and dry them thoroughly.

Put the shredded cabbage in a large bowl with the kidney beans, onion and beetroot. Mix well. Whisk together all the ingredients for the walnut vinaigrette. Pour over the salad and toss well.

Line a large salad bowl with the radicchio leaves. Pile the salad in the centre and sprinkle the Stilton and poppy seeds over the top.

Mushroom Ratatouille Salad

Serves 8 as a side dish

Working time: about 30 minutes

Total time: about 2 hours and 15 minutes

Calories 75
Protein 3g
Cholesterol 0mg
Total fat 4g
Saturated fat 1g
Sodium 110mg

750g	aubergines, cut into 2 cm (¾ inch) pieces	**1½ lb**	**2**	sweet yellow peppers, blanched and cut into 6 cm (2½ inch) long strips	**2**
1½ tsp	salt	**1½ tsp**	**500 g**	Italian plum tomatoes, skinned, seeded and roughly chopped into 1 cm (½ inch) pieces	**1 lb**
2 tbsp	virgin olive oil	**2 tbsp**			
2	large onions, cut into fine rings	**2**		freshly ground black pepper	
4	garlic cloves crushed	**4**	**3 tbsp**	chopped parsley	**3 tbsp**
4 tbsp	white wine	**4 tbsp**			
250g	chestnut mushrooms, sliced	**8 oz**			
3 tbsp	chopped fresh oregano	**3 tbsp**			

In a bowl, toss the aubergine pieces with 1 teaspoon of the salt. Place the aubergine in a colander and weight it down with a plate small enough to rest on top of the pieces. Let the aubergine drain for 30 minutes, to eliminate its natural bitterness. Rinse the aubergine under cold running water to rid it of the salt, and drain it well. Pat the pieces dry on paper towels.

Heat the oil in a large saucepan. Add the onion and cook it over low heat for about 8 minutes, stirring occasionally, until it is soft but not brown. Mix in the garlic and cook for a further minute. Add the aubergine pieces to the saucepan, pour in the wine and cook them, uncovered, for 15 minutes. Stir in the mushroom slices and the oregano, cover the pan, and cook the mixture for 5 minutes more.

Remove the lid from the pan and add the yellow pepper strips, the tomatoes, the remaining salt and some freshly ground black pepper. Heat the contents through for 2 minutes, stir in the parsley, and set the pan aside for the salad to cool.

Transfer to a salad bowl and serve.

Green and White Rice Salad

Serves 12 as a
side dish

Working time:
about 25
minutes

Total time:
about 45
minutes

Calories
105
Protein
2g
Cholesterol
0mg
Total fat
5g
Saturated fat
1g
Sodium
123mg

45 cl	unsalted vegetable stock	**¾ pint**
175 g	long-grain rice	**6 oz**
400 g	fresh peas, shelled, or 125 g (4 oz) frozen peas	**14 oz**
½	cucumber, cut into 5 mm (¼ inch) dice	**½**
125 g	courgettes, trimmed and julienned	**4 oz**
6	spring onions, trimmed and thinly sliced diagonally	**6**
1 tbsp	finely cut chives	**1 tbsp**

3 tbsp	chopped parsley	**3 tbsp**
1	crisp round lettuce, leaves washed and dried	**1**
	Tarragon vinaigrette	
½ tsp	French mustard	**½ tsp**
⅛ tsp	salt	**⅛ tsp**
⅛ tsp	freshly ground black pepper	**⅛ tsp**
2 tbsp	tarragon vinegar	**2 tbsp**
4 tbsp	walnut or virgin olive oil	**4 tbsp**

Bring the stock to the boil and add the rice. Reduce to a simmer and cook covered, until just tender and all the stock is absorbed—15 to 20 minutes. Set aside.

Blanch the fresh peas in boiling water for about 30 seconds; if using frozen peas, add them to boiling water and just bring back to the boil. Drain the peas, refresh under cold water and drain again.

Transfer the cooled rice to a large bowl, add the blanched peas, the cucumber and the courgettes, and mix the ingredients together well. Stir in the spring onion slices, the chives and the parsley.

To make the dressing, whisk the mustard, salt, black pepper, vinegar and oil together in a small bowl. Pour the dressing over the salad, and toss it thoroughly. Chill it in the refrigerator until ready to serve.

To serve, line a large serving bowl with the lettuce leaves and pile the salad in the centre.

Sweet Pepper Rice Ring

Serves 6

Working time:
about 30
minutes

Total time:
about 1 hour

Calories
125
Protein
3g
Cholesterol
0mg
Total fat
3g
Saturated fat
1g
Sodium
135mg

½ tsp	salt	½ tsp
150 g	long-grain rice	5 oz
1	small sweet red pepper	1
1	small sweet green pepper	1
1	small sweet yellow pepper	1
1 tbsp	virgin olive oil	1 tbsp

1 tbsp	white wine vinegar	1 tbsp
1	garlic clove, crushed	1
4 tbsp	finely chopped parsley	4 tbsp
	freshly ground black pepper	
	red, green and yellow pepper	
	rings, for garnish	

Bring a saucepan of water to the boil with ¼ teaspoon of the salt. Add the rice, stir it once, then cover the pan and reduce the heat to low. Simmer the rice for 20 minutes, until it is cooked but still slightly firm. Drain it thoroughly and set it aside to cool.

Meanwhile, skin the peppers, then seed and derib them, retaining their juice. Cut the peppers into small dice.

Put the oil, vinegar, garlic and parsley into a large bowl, and add the remaining salt and some pepper. Mix the ingredients well. Add the diced peppers to the dressing, with 1 tablespoon of their juice, then add the rice and mix everything together thoroughly. Fill a 1.25 litre (2 pint) ring mould with the rice salad, pressing the mixture down firmly. Cover the mould with plastic film and refrigerate until ready to serve.

To serve, turn the rice salad out on to a serving plate and arrange the pepper rings in the centre.

Charcoal-Grilled Summer Salad

Serves 8 as a side dish

Working time: about 1 hour

Total time: about 1 hour and 30 minutes

Calories 95
Protein 3g
Cholesterol 0mg
Total fat 5g
Saturated fat 1g
Sodium 115mg

1	large aubergine	1
½ tsp	salt	½ tsp
2	large courgettes	2
½ tsp	virgin olive oil	½ tsp
	freshly ground black pepper	
2	sweet red peppers	2
250 g	Batavian endive or rocket	8 oz
4	ripe tomatoes, halved lengthwise	4
1	small red onion, very thinly sliced	1

Garlic and herb dressing

1	whole garlic bulb, top cut off	1
5 tsp	virgin olive oil	5 tsp
1 tbsp	fresh lemon juice	1 tbsp
1 tbsp	chopped fresh parsley	1 tbsp
½ tsp	fresh thyme	½ tsp
½ tbsp	chopped fresh oregano	½ tbsp
⅛ tsp	salt	⅛ tsp
	freshly ground black pepper	
1 tbsp	walnut or safflower oil	1 tbsp

Preheat the oven to 180°C (350°F or Mark 4). Dribble ½ tsp olive oil onto the garlic and roast it wrapped in foil, until soft—1 hour. Half way through roasting, light the barbecue. When cool enough, skin the garlic cloves and set aside.

Peel the aubergine and cut lengthwise into eight. Sprinkle on ½ tsp of salt for 30 minutes. Rinse and pat dry. Cut the courgettes into four slices. Brush the aubergine and courgette with ½ tsp oil. Sprinkle with pepper and set aside.

When the charcoal is hot, grill the red peppers on the rack, until blistered on all sides. Transfer to a bowl and cover with plastic film to loosen the skins.

Grill the aubergine and courgette until golden. Remove from the barbecue and cool.

Peel the peppers. Quarter and seed, then set aside.

Press the garlic through a sieve into a bowl. Add the lemon juice, herbs and seasoning; stir well. Whisking, pour in the remaining oils in a steady stream and whisk until combined.

Arrange the endive on a large platter. Position the vegetables on top. Pour dressing on and serve.

Barbecued Bananas with Raspberry Coulis

Serves 8

Working (and total) time: about 20 minutes

Calories 110
Protein 3g
Cholesterol 0mg
Total fat trace
Saturated fat trace
Sodium 10mg

200 g	fresh raspberries, or frozen raspberries, thawed	**7 oz**
2 tbsp	icing sugar	**2 tbsp**
½ tsp	arrowroot	**½ tsp**
2 tbsp	passion fruits, strained juice only or Kirsch	**2 tbsp** **2**
8	ripe large bananas	**8**

In a blender or food processor, blend the raspberries with the icing sugar until they are reduced to a purée. Press the purée through a nylon sieve to remove all the seeds, then pour it into a saucepan. Stir the arrowroot into the purée and heat it gently, stirring continuously, until it boils and thickens. Remove the pan from the heat and stir in the passion fruit juice or Kirsch. Either cover the sauce and keep it warm or set it aside to cool while you barbecue the bananas.

With a sharp knife point, cut the skin along the length of a banana in two places on opposite sides; do not cut into the flesh. Peel off the top half of the skin, leaving the flesh and bottom half of the skin intact. Half-peel the remaining bananas in the same way.

Place the bananas, skin side down, on the barbecue rack, 10 to 15 cm (4 to 6 inches) above medium-hot coals. When the skins have blackened—after about 5 minutes—carefully turn the bananas over and cook them for a further minute.

Serve the bananas hot, in their skins, with a little of the raspberry coulis—either hot or cold—poured over them. Serve the remaining coulis separately.

Baked Apples with Ginger

Serves 8

Working time:
about 30
minutes

Total time:
about 1 hour
and 15
minutes

Calories
165
Protein
2g
Cholesterol
5mg
Total fat
3g
Saturated fat
1g
Sodium
85mg

8	firm eating apples (about 150 g/5 oz each)	**8**
100 g	peeled cooked chestnuts or shelled hazelnuts, roughly chopped	**3 ½ oz**
75 g	fresh wholemeal breadcrumbs	**2 ½ oz**
60 g	seedless raisins, chopped if large	**2 oz**
30 g	stem ginger, finely diced	**1 oz**
2 tbsp	fresh lemon juice	**2 tbsp**
2 tbsp	maple syrup	**2 tbsp**
1 tsp	ground mixed spice	**1 tsp**
15 g	unsalted butter, melted	**½ oz**
125 g	thick Greek yogurt (optional)	**4 oz**

Wash the apples and core them, making the hole through the centre of the apple about 2.5 cm (1 inch) in diameter. Keeping the apples whole, score the skin round the circumference of each with a sharp knife.

Place the chestnuts, breadcrumbs, seedless raisins, ginger, lemon juice, maple syrup and mixed spice in a large bowl. Knead these ingredients lightly with one hand to amalgamate them.

Cut eight squares of foil, each one large enough to wrap round an apple. Brush one side of the foil squares with the melted butter. Place an apple in the centre of the buttered side of each foil square, and press an eighth of the stuffing into the hollowed centre of the apple. Wrap the apples in the foil.

Arrange the wrapped apples on the rack over medium-hot coals and cook them for about 45 minutes. Test the apples by piercing them with a thin skewer: if it meets little resistance, they are done.

Serve the baked apples hot, with a little thick Greek yogurt, if you are using it.

Mixed Berry Yogurt Ice

Serves 10

Working time:
about 40
minutes

Total time:
about 11 hours
(includes
freezing)

Calories
200
Protein
5g
Cholesterol
0mg
Total fat
1g
Saturated fat
trace
Sodium
65mg

750 g	mixed soft fruits (blackberries, strawberries, blueberries, raspberries, blackcurrants, redcurrants), hulled, stemmed or picked over, as appropriate	**1½ lb**	
350 g	caster sugar	**12 oz**	
3	egg whites	**3**	
60 cl	plain low-fat yogurt	**1 pint**	
2 tbsp	Kirsch	**2 tbsp**	

Purée the soft fruits in a food processor. Pass the purée through a nylon sieve and set it aside.

Put 15 cl (¼ pint) of water and the sugar into a heavy-bottomed saucepan. Set the pan over medium heat and stir the mixture gently with a wooden spoon to dissolve the sugar; brush down any sugar crystals stuck to the sides of the pan with a pastry brush dipped in hot water. Warm a sugar thermometer in a jug of hot water and place it in the pan. Increase the heat, bring the syrup to the boil, and continue to boil it rapidly until the temperature on the thermometer is between 121°C and 130°C (250°F and 266°F).

While the syrup is cooking, whisk the egg whites in a bowl until they form stiff peaks. Whisking all the time, pour the boiling sugar

syrup into the egg whites in a thin, steady stream. Continue to whisk the meringue mixture vigorously until it is cool—about 10 minutes—then set it aside for 5 minutes to cool completely.

Measure off 35 cl (12 fl oz) of the fruit purée. Transfer the remaining purée to a sealed plastic container and refrigerate. Using a metal tablespoon, carefully fold the measured fruit purée into the cooled meringue, then fold in the yogurt and the Kirsch. Turn the mixture into a rigid plastic container, smooth it level and cover it with a lid. Place in the freezer, which should be set as low as possible, and leave the mixture to set—10 to 12 hours. When ready to serve, remove from the freezer and serve with the fruit purée.

Fresh Fruits in a Watermelon Bowl

Serves 8

Working time:
about 45
minutes

Total time
about 2 hours
(includes
chilling)

Calories
80

Protein
2g

Cholesterol
0mg

Total fat
0g

Saturated fat
0g

Sodium
10mg

1	watermelon (about 3 kg/6 $\frac{1}{2}$ lb)	1
6	ripe figs, washed, stemmed and cut lengthwise into eighths	6
250g	seedless red grapes, washed and stemmed	8 oz

2	oranges, juice and grated rind	2
1	lemon, grated rind only	1
1 tbsp	ginger syrup, from a jar of preserved stem ginger	1 tbsp
2 tbsp	clear honey	2 tbsp

Slice off the top of the watermelon, about one fifth of the way down. Scoop out the flesh from the lid. Remove the seeds and cut the flesh into 2.5 cm (1 inch) chunks. Reserve the lid.

Run a long-bladed knife round the edge of the large piece of melon, between the flesh and the skin, cutting down deeply and keeping as close as possible to the skin. Make a series of deep parallel cuts, 2.5 cm (1 inch) apart, across the flesh, followed by a series of similar cuts at right angles to the first. Gently scoop out the long, square sections of flesh. Remove the seeds and chop the flesh into cubes. Scrape the remaining flesh from the

walls of the watermelon shell, then seed it and cut it into pieces. Reserve the shell. Put all the pieces of watermelon flesh into a large, heatproof bowl and add the figs and grapes.

In a small pan, mix together the orange juice and rind, the lemon rind, the ginger syrup and the honey. Bring slowly to the boil and pour over the fruit. Stir the fruit and syrup together, then leave to cool for 5 minutes. Stir again, cover and chill for 1 hour. Turn the fruit over occasionally, it to absorb the syrup.

To serve the salad, transfer the chilled fruit to the watermelon shell, replace the lid and place on a platter.

Kebabs in Tea and Ginger Marinade

Serves 4

Working time: about 35 minutes

Total time: about 9 hours (includes marinating)

Calories 160
Protein 22g
Cholesterol 70mg
Total fat 8g
Saturated fat 3g

500g	pork fillet, trimmed of fat and cut into 24 cubes	**1 lb**
16	shallots, peeled, or spring onion bulbs	**16**
16	button mushrooms	**16**

Tea marinade

1 tsp	Earl Grey tea leaves	**1 tsp**
1	garlic clove, crushed	**1**
2 tbsp	finely chopped fresh ginger root	**2 tbsp**
4 tbsp	dry sherry	**4 tbsp**
1 tbsp	light brown sugar	**1 tbsp**
2 tbsp	virgin olive oil	**2 tbsp**

To make the marinade, put the tea leaves in a jug and pour 12.5 cl (4 fl oz) of boiling water over the leaves. Leave to steep for 4 minutes, then strain into a bowl. Add the remaining marinade ingredients to the bowl and stir to mix well.

Add the pork cubes to the bowl and turn to coat with the marinade. Cover the bowl and put it in the refrigerator for 8 hours, or overnight.

When ready to cook, preheat the grill. Drain the meat, reserving the marinade. Thread the pork cubes alternating with the shallots and mushrooms on to eight skewers. Brush all over with the marinade and grill, about 12.5 cm (5 inches) from the source of heat, for 15 minutes, turning to cook evenly and basting frequently with the reserved marinade. Serve hot.

Editor's Note: If you use wooden skewers, soak them in water for about 10 minutes before threading them with the pork and vegetables to prevent them from burning under the grill.

Porkburgers

Serves 4

Working (and total) time about 35 minutes

Calories 340
Protein 32g
Cholesterol 85mg
Total fat 12g
Saturated fat 4g
Sodium 550mg

250 g	pork fillet, trimmed of fat and minced	8 oz
250 g	topside of veal, trimmed of fat and minced	8 oz
1	onion, very finely chopped	1
$\frac{1}{4}$ tsp	salt	$\frac{1}{4}$ tsp
$\frac{1}{2}$ tsp	dry mustard	$\frac{1}{2}$ tsp
$\frac{1}{4}$ tsp	chili powder	$\frac{1}{4}$ tsp
1 tbsp	safflower oil	1 tbsp
4	wholemeal baps, split in half	4

4	crisp lettuce leaves, washed and dried	4
4	slices beef tomato	4
4	mild or hot pickled chili peppers	4
	Chili topping	
4 tbsp	chili relish	4 tbsp
	carrot, grated	
2	shallots, finely chopped	2
2.5cm	piece cucumber, finely chopped	1 inch

In a bowl, mix the pork with the veal, onion, salt, dry mustard and chili powder. Form the mixture into four burger shapes about 1 cm ($\frac{1}{2}$ inch) thick.

Heat the oil in a large heavy frying pan over medium heat. Add the porkburgers and cook them for 5 to 6 minutes on each side.

Meanwhile, make the topping. In a bowl, mix the chili relish with the carrot, shallots and cucumber. Warm the baps under a medium-hot grill.

Arrange a lettuce leaf on the base portion of each bap, then add a porkburger to each, and top with a slice of tomato and a spoonful of chili topping. Cover with the bap lids and secure them in position with cocktail sticks. Garnish the burgers with the pickled chili peppers, and serve at once.

Useful weights and measures

Weight Equivalents

Avoirdupois		Metric
1 ounce	=	28.35 grams
1 pound	=	254.6 grams
2.3 pounds	=	1 kilogram

Liquid Measurements

$^1/_4$ pint	=	$1^1/_2$ decilitres
$^1/_2$ pint	=	$^1/_4$ litre
scant 1 pint	=	$^1/_2$ litre
$1^3/_4$ pints	=	1 litre
1 gallon	=	4.5 litres

Liquid Measures

1 pint	=	20 fl oz	=	32 tablespoons
$^1/_2$ pint	=	10 fl oz	=	16 tablespoons
$^1/_4$ pint	=	5 fl oz	=	8 tablespoons
$^1/_8$ pint	=	$2^1/_2$ fl oz	=	4 tablespoons
$^1/_{16}$ pint	=	$1^1/_4$ fl oz	=	2 tablespoons

Solid Measures

1 oz almonds, ground = $3^3/_4$ level tablespoons
1 oz breadcrumbs fresh = 7 level tablespoons
1 oz butter, lard = 2 level tablespoons
1 oz cheese, grated = $3^1/_2$ level tablespoons
1 oz cocoa = $2^3/_4$ level tablespoons
1 oz desiccated coconut = $4^1/_2$ tablespoons
1 oz cornflour = $2^1/_2$ tablespoons
1 oz custard powder = $2^1/_2$ tablespoons
1 oz curry powder and spices = 5 tablespoons
1 oz flour = 2 level tablespoons
1 oz rice, uncooked = $1^1/_2$ tablespoons
1 oz sugar, caster and granulated = 2 tablespoons
1 oz icing sugar = $2^1/_2$ tablespoons
1 oz yeast, granulated = 1 level tablespoon

American Measures

16 fl oz	=1 American pint
8 fl oz	=1 American standard cup
0.50 fl oz	=1 American tablespoon

(*slightly smaller than British Standards Institute tablespoon*)

0.16 fl oz	=1 American teaspoon

Australian Cup Measures

(*Using the 8-liquid-ounce cup measure*)

1 cup flour	4 oz
1 cup sugar (crystal or caster)	8 oz
1 cup icing sugar (free from lumps)	5 oz
1 cup shortening (butter, margarine)	8 oz
1 cup brown sugar (lightly packed)	4 oz
1 cup soft breadcrumbs	2 oz
1 cup dry breadcrumbs	3 oz
1 cup rice (uncooked)	6 oz
1 cup rice (cooked)	5 oz
1 cup mixed fruit	4 oz
1 cup grated cheese	4 oz
1 cup nuts (chopped)	4 oz
1 cup coconut	$2^1/_2$ oz

Australian Spoon Measures

	level tablespoon
1 oz flour	2
1 oz sugar	$1^1/_2$
1 oz icing sugar	2
1 oz shortening	1
1 oz honey	1
1 oz gelatine	2
1 oz cocoa	3
1 oz cornflour	$2^1/_2$
1 oz custard powder	$2^1/_2$

Australian Liquid Measures

(*Using 8-liquid-ounce cup*)

1 cup liquid	8 oz
$2^1/_2$ cups liquid	20 oz (1 pint)
2 tablespoons liquid	1 oz
1 gill liquid	5 oz ($^1/_4$ pint)